Miracle Children

Behavior and Learning Difficulties Uprooted

Anna R. Buck

Published by Anna's House, LLC
Broomfield, Colorado

The stories in this book are true,
although the names have been changed.

Miracle Children: Behavior and Learning Difficulties Uprooted

First edition:
ISBN 978-0-9814796-0-6

Library of Congress Control Number: 2008900233

Published by Anna's House, LLC
Broomfield, Colorado

www.AnnasHouseLLC.com

Editor: Evie Hemphill
Cover Design: Cathi Stevenson
Cover images copyright Adobe Systems Inc. and licensors
Illustrator: Denis Proulx
Photograph of author: Timothy M. Smith
Printed in Canada by Friesens

Acknowledgements

I am deeply grateful for my wonderful husband, Robert, who has been so patient with the time and energy that has consumed me in this project. Thanks to Jimmy and Melissa for their continued words of encouragement.

Pat Hale, thank you for challenging me to explain my work simply and for the time you volunteered to read and re-read and correct my many errors. Your critiques throughout the process have been greatly appreciated.

Thank you, Kristin Wright-Bettner, for your volunteered time to read and offer insightful and outstanding suggestions.

Evie Hemphill, thank you for the numerous hours you spent editing and fine-tuning my writing.

Paul Madaule and Sophie Garceau of The Listening Centre—as well as The Listening Centre staff—and Peter Blythe and Sally Goddard Blythe of INPP, thank you for the excellent training and support.

And finally, thank you to the parents who so openly and graciously shared their children's stories. You made this book possible.

To Anna Lee

"I will praise You, for I am fearfully and wonderfully made"
Psalm 139:14

Contents

Foreword

In my library I have thousands of books on the brain—the brain-body connection, Specific Learning Disabilities, Dyslexia, Developmental Coordination Disorder (Dyspraxia), Attention Deficit Disorder (ADD), Attention Deficit Hyperactivity Disorder (ADHD), Behaviour Disorders and Developmental Delay, Neurology, Psychology, Autistic Spectrum Disorders—*but this book is unique.*

I consider *Miracle Children* a book that tens of thousands of parents throughout the Western world have been waiting for, because it proves that their dreams and hopes as parents can become reality.

It is the dream of every parent that their children will be happy and free from any behavioural problems or difficulties at school. But far too often their child, who is obviously intelligent, cannot show his or her intelligence in an acceptable academic way in the classroom, or behave like other children of the same age. The author, Anna Buck, had such a daughter. As a result she spent years, and a lot of money, trying to find what was causing her daughter's problems and getting her daughter to try a variety of interventions to solve her difficulties.

They all failed. Eventually all her efforts and searching paid off. She ultimately found two non-invasive answers. One of these involved her making the long journey to Chester, England, and studying Neuro-Developmental Delay with Sally Goddard Blythe at The Institute for Neuro-Physiological Psychology (INPP), and then returning home to work with her daughter.

The first part of this book tells how Neuro-Developmental Delay Therapy, as practiced by INPP practitioners, solved her daughter's problems and allowed her to change beyond her wildest dreams. And changed she really is. I know, because I have had the pleasure of meeting her daughter—a young, normal and attractive lady; and it was only some months later, and after reading *Miracle Children,* that I discovered just how severe her difficulties had been.

Once Anna found the answers and resolved her daughter's difficulties, she wanted to prove to herself, and to thousands of other parents, that what her daughter had achieved could also be achieved by other children who have problems with educational achievement and/or emotional difficulties. This she has done, and this book gives some of the many case histories that she has in her files—stories of children who underwent such amazing and positive changes that their parents considered them to be "miraculous."

If I have given the impression that this is a book for parents alone, that would be wrong; it is also a book for all professionals working with children who have Specific Learning Disabilities, coordination disorders, behavioural problems and so forth. To date many professionals have worked hard and long with children like the "miracle children," but with minimum success; and that, they know all too well, is very dispiriting. This book will introduce them to two systems that have been proven to work.

--Peter Blythe, founder and director of The Institute for Neuro-Physiological Psychology from 1975-2001

My Own Miracle Child

I was a frustrated mother; she was a highly frustrated child. We were tired of endless evaluations by reading, educational, physical and visual specialists. We tried vision therapy, specialized reading programs, herbal supplements and specialized diets. Although they slightly relieved some of the symptoms, they were not solutions. Nothing changed her foremost symptoms of Dyslexia and Dyspraxia. The message we heard over and over again was that we needed to accept and cope with her disabilities. I was discouraged and aggravated. I wanted answers, and I was not willing to teach my daughter to cope with "disabilities" it seemed no one understood.

I spent countless hours reading, researching and observing. A long-time tutor, I began recognizing specific problems in several of the children I worked with that resembled some of the many I saw in my own child. I wondered if there might have been a primary cause such as a glitch, chemical reaction or some sort of defect in the brain. Although most of the children I had tutored over the previous 20-plus years had been through occupational therapy, physical therapy, speech therapy, vision therapy, sensory integration, and so forth, these same children continued to struggle with their difficulties: gross and fine motor skills, speech and language, poor eye movements, academics and behavior. Many of these children showed flawless eye movements (i.e., eye tracking and convergence) when they graduated from vision therapy, but as soon as I engaged them in reading or writing, their eye movements became erratic and faulty. I noticed distinguishing similarities in behavior and learning problems among the wide-ranging difficulties and diagnoses these children experience.

Like many of the children I tutored, my daughter was not only a puzzle to me, but to nearly everyone we encountered. She struggled with uncontrollable fear, anger, balance, orientation and spatial awareness, understanding concrete versus abstract, rhythm, tactile sensitivities, speech and language skills, gross and fine motor skills, eye movements, academics—just about everything. She struggled with adapting to change and social interactions. It was as if she did not want others to notice, acknowledge or approach her in any way, and she habitually avoided eye contact.

She had always been an obedient child who consistently sought to do what was right, and I was never overly concerned about decisions she might make. She rarely, if ever, made any decisions on her own. Household rules were established, and she followed them precisely. However, if she was troubled or frightened in any way, no amount of reasoning could change her mind or persuade her otherwise.

She was consumed by her fears. Whenever I took her somewhere, even the familiar home of another family, and encouraged her to go play with the other children, she was often too fearful to do so. Typically she played well by herself even if other children were present, as long as I remained within eyesight. If the surroundings were unfamiliar to her or uncomfortable for her in any way, she hovered and clung to me no matter how enticing the toys might have been. No amount of reasoning could change her mind. If we were in a large-group setting, she clung to me as if wanting to completely disappear. If someone approached her just to say "hi," she did not speak. It was difficult to pin down exactly what her fears were. But gradually I started to identify them as I closely observed and analyzed her behavior.

I did not understand why, but it was evident that fear dominated her life in many ways, including daily and routine activities. She was afraid of water, so I kept her bathwater very shallow. She never put her head in the water and even resisted a washcloth coming close to her face. Trying to wash her hair required such physical exertion on my part that I avoided it until it was extremely necessary. Each time, I laid her on her back on the kitchen counter and then held her head over the sink and promised I wouldn't let the water touch her face. Then I filled a glass with water and slowly and gently poured it over the back of her hair. During the entire process her body remained extremely tight and rigid, the look in her eyes was of extreme fear, and her neck felt stiff and hard— like a block of wood. If the water came remotely close to her face, she immediately jerked her head upright, flailed her arms and legs and started crying frantically.

It worried me that she was afraid not only of water, but also of seemingly harmless objects. Every time I took our car through a brush carwash, she screamed and frantically jumped up and down. It was obvious to me that she was not having a temper tantrum; she was petrified. I was unable to calm her, even if I held her in my lap and covered her eyes. She did not calm down until we were completely out of the carwash. On one particular occasion she told me she was convinced the brushes were coming toward her and they were going to swallow her up. She could not understand that the brushes were outside of the car, and any explaining I provided did not convince her otherwise.

My daughter's fears created unusually strong-willed and stubborn behavior. Her Sunday School teacher told me she was, at age three, "quite a little stinker." She said my daughter was polite and obedient, but if she did not want to participate in an activity, no amount of reasoning or persuasion could change her mind. I was told over and over how stubborn and strong-willed my child was.

My daughter's overwhelming fears included extreme distrust of others. She physically fought against and resisted doctors regardless of the situation. One day she scratched the cornea of her eye. The doctor wanted to put a drop of dye in her eye to ascertain the extent of the injury, but as soon as he got near, my daughter began screaming and flailing her arms and legs. The doctor left the room and returned with three adult assistants—two men and one woman. It took all four of them to hold down my seven-year-old so he could put one drop in her eye. Afterward the doctor said, "Eeesh! I should get combat pay for that!" On another occasion it took three adults at the dentist's office to hold her down in order to administer one shot for a small filling. When she was in vision therapy, the optometrist was often frustrated with her lack of response to questions. The doctor continually repeated, "I cannot hear you," or "You need to give me an answer." Each time I was humiliated and mortified. I was sure people believed that I did not discipline my child or teach her appropriate behavior. Aside from those feelings, I wondered what could possibly be happening that could create such obstinacy and fear in a child.

She was highly emotional and volatile. She displayed drastic mood swings and seemed angry or belligerent most of the time. When her anger surfaced, seemingly out of nowhere, it was impossible to reason with her. During these moods she became irrational, and nothing could snap her out of it. On several occasions her anger was so intense that she grabbed scissors and cut holes in the clothes she was wearing. Various friends suggested I needed to implement better parenting techniques, and I knew they did not understand what we were experiencing. It was quite disconcerting to hear her say she wished she was dead. Another doctor suggested she suffered with both Dyslexia and Bipolar disorder. I was angry. A label means "learn to cope." I was not interested in labels. I wanted answers.

When my daughter was about seven years old, a friend of mine said he was convinced that this was not a parenting problem, but some sort of chemical imbalance in the brain. He recommended some supplements and tinctures. Overall I found them to be ineffective. We might have experienced very short periods of settled, calmer behavior, but the problems continued. Her sister called the supplements her "monster medicine" because they eased the belligerence. In a very short time, however, the belligerent and irrational behavior surfaced again. I learned that her belligerence and irrationality were based on fear. Yet nothing we would say or do could change her mind or alleviate her fears. She could not be soothed.

She showed poor balance and could not anticipate response to movement. At eight years old she still could not ride a bicycle—she had a fear of learning how to do it as well as an inability to balance. She could not anticipate movement for balance. Most of us take for granted the seemingly natural anticipation of and response to movement, such as how our bodies move on bicycles as we turn corners, or how we counter the movement of a raft on a river, or how we move our bodies to balance on a balance beam. She was completely unable to balance her body. Anything that might alter her sense of balance frightened her because she lacked the ability to anticipate and respond to stimuli.

Orientation and spatial awareness were deficient. It was as if she was not quite certain where she was in relation to her surroundings, or where objects were in relation to her own body. Left versus right, directions and understanding her bearings in a store or location away from home were foreign to her. She miscalculated doorways and walked into walls, corners and furniture. She often walked the house during the night. I frequently heard her feet as she roamed the house, room to room, for an hour or more at a time, and I would finally relax when I heard her return to her bed. Each time I asked her about it the next morning, and her response was always the same—she couldn't sleep and had wandered about as something to do. She would not play on swings or go down slides. Occasionally I tried to convince her that I would stand at the bottom of a slide at the park and catch her as she came down. Instead of a response such as, "I don't want to do that," she would give me a look of sheer terror and then scream and run from me.

She could not distinguish between reality and fantasy, between concrete and abstract. She could pretend in her play, but she could not form mental images. It was as if she lacked the capacity to visualize or create things in her mind without the aid of dolls or toys. Even after extensive vision therapy she still could not do this. Cartoons on the television triggered emotional reactions. It disturbed me immensely as I watched her recoil against the back of the couch during an "intense" scene in a cartoon. She cried whenever a cartoon character was injured. I could not explain to her, even at the age of eight or nine, that what she was watching was not real. I learned to monitor which cartoons she could watch as much as I did television shows.

She was incapable of demonstrating rhythm in body movements, speech or songs. She could not recite a very short poem with any sense of rhythm or sing along with children's songs. It was impossible for her to get one word out before the song was several lines ahead of her. Attempts at teaching her hand or body motions to songs were absolutely hopeless. She could not follow stories when they were read to her. She could not repeat a story in any kind of sequence. She could not repeat verbatim a very short Bible verse for Sunday School. Her inability to clearly articulate or say complete words or sentences made it difficult to understand her in almost all of her attempts to communicate. Answering the phone became problematic because she could not repeat a message or a phone number accurately. Her response time to questions asked over the phone was extremely slow, and when she brought the phone to me she had no idea who was on the line or what the person had said.

I had asked a speech pathologist friend to evaluate her when she was six years old. The report came back that she did show speech delay, but it was not considered significant; and I was told that she would probably outgrow it. It seemed to me she had a more encompassing problem, and speech difficulty was just one of many symptoms. Within the next two years her voice became softer and softer and her mumbling increased, and soon no one could understand her. She increasingly withdrew inside herself. She did not respond when spoken to, and when she did respond it was with anger. She did not engage in social activities or conversations; she preferred playing alone with her toys without being disturbed.

My daughter's tactile sensitivities were abnormal. She did not like to be touched or hugged in any way. She lacked the ability to feel pain or sickness. Usually I was completely unaware of her illnesses until I saw the runny nose, heard a terrible cough or realized she was vomiting. She never vocalized tummy aches, sore throats or other common childhood conditions. One time she reached up and touched a hot burner while her grandmother was cooking. Her finger blistered yet she never shed a tear. She always wore socks, even on the hottest summer days. She hated clothes fitting her at the waist—the baggier the better.

Her gross and fine motor skills were deficient. She was noticeably uncoordinated and awkward in movements. When she ran across a playground it looked as if she was running in place. She ran as hard as she could, and it seemed she barely advanced. The left side of her body did not participate in movement to the same degree as the right side. Her arms and legs did not cross the midline of her body. She never sat cross-legged, and she never crossed her arms. Her limbs could come to the center symmetry-line of her body, but they did not naturally or instinctively cross the line. Her fine motor skills were absent. Although she could hold a pencil, coordination of the pencil was difficult. She could not deal cards when playing card games without taking a prolonged amount of time to separate each card. She could not count cards while dealing hands.

When it came time to start academics, she could not remember day-to-day what she had supposedly learned the previous day. It was an impossible task trying to teach her the letters and sounds of the alphabet. When I made the sound of a specific letter, she could not accurately repeat the sound back to me, particularly the vowel sounds. I had her hearing checked, and the audiogram came back as normal.

Spelling and writing were atrocious and seemingly pointless activities. I knew my daughter was intelligent, but she was unable to demonstrate it academically. What she did write was illegible, and if I asked her to read it back to me, she could not. Her first-grade teacher, in her only year as a nonhome-schooled student, insisted that she was highly dysfunctional and suffered from significant learning disabilities. I was angry, offended and certain that the woman had no insight whatsoever as to my daughter's intelligence or abilities. It was clear to me that something was blocking her ability to function physically and mentally.

She could not learn to read, and I was at a loss to understand why. An optometrist found that her eyes were not able to track, nor could they converge. She was lacking in eye accommodation skills, depth perception and peripheral vision. As an eight-year-old she began 18 months of vision therapy. When completed, the optometrist said her eye movements were beautiful. She was a bit more coordinated, yet she still could not read or write. Her writing showed poor spacing, omissions and reversals. I was frustrated that all her work in vision therapy had not solved her eye problems. She could track with her eyes as long as she did not have to engage in any reading or cognitive processing. As soon as she attempted to decode words, apply comprehension skills, read, write or copy, eye tracking and convergence disappeared.

I investigated various reading and specialized academic programs. She spent 18 months at a reading center that guaranteed they could teach her to read during that time or the program would be free. Eighteen months came and went, and they graduated her at the age of 14, even though she still could not read beyond third-grade level. I fought them on their guarantee, but they said she was reading as well as she ever would. A private, specialized school tested her and offered to take her as a student for $15,000 per year. When they showed me their program, which was structured on traditional teaching through rote, I was aghast. My daughter could not accurately repeat one simple sentence. How could she be expected to learn through rote teaching? I shared with the school what I had been doing with her academically at home, and they said I was doing the best that could probably be done for her.

These problems continued into her teenage years. When we went to department stores she never wanted to be separated from me. I later learned it was because she was unable to orient herself. Even though we routinely frequented the same stores, she did not know how to get to specific departments, and then she did not know how she could later find me again.

Because she has always had a love for horses and animals, I signed her up for horseback riding lessons when she was 17. Unfortunately, the instructor struggled with patience as she tried to coach my daughter. The necessary rhythm was nonexistent. The instructor would tell her to move her legs a certain way and lift her bottom off the saddle in a certain manner, and it looked as if she had no idea how to make her body parts cooperate. One day I suddenly realized, "Oh, my gosh! She doesn't even know where her own derrière is!"

As a teenager in a restaurant, she could not read menus. I tried to protect her from embarrassment by intentionally sitting next to her and discussing the menu items with her so that she could make a decision. Then I ordered for her because she was uncomfortable speaking up and ordering for herself. I think she was fully aware that her voice was too soft to be heard, but I think she also feared she would not be able to accurately articulate what she wanted to say.

She could not count money. When she made purchases with her own money, I stood next to her and tried to protect her from embarrassment by asserting myself and verbally suggesting she was having an off day to the cashier. Then I offered to help her count out her money. Or, I hurriedly added her items mentally and then told her which bills to give the cashier and whether or not to expect change.

Ultimately, after years of extreme frustration, I realized it was up to me to determine the root of her problems. I had seen similar but milder issues again and again in children I tutored; I knew I was not alone, even though I felt very alone. After 10 years of research, I concluded the root problem for my daughter, and for many of the children I tutored, lay in dysfunctions within the central nervous system, beginning with the brain stem. Research led me to two schools: The Institute for Neuro-Physiological Psychology (INPP) in Chester, U.K., and The Listening Centre in Toronto, Ontario, Canada.

I chose INPP because I saw that I could go to the original source for thorough training in this field. Many individuals and organizations have branched off with various methods for treatment, but Neuro-Developmental Delay (NDD) Therapy originally came from the work of INPP founder Dr. Peter Blythe. I wanted to learn directly from him (although he has officially retired) and from the current director of INPP, Sally Goddard Blythe. I chose The Listening Centre because it is similarly based on human developmental growth, and the microphone work during part of the therapy results in significant changes that I doubted I would find in any other sound program.

Training at The Institute for Neuro-Physiological Psychology and The Listening Centre together provided the missing links. I saw opportunity for optimum results by appropriately implementing both treatment programs. After my training and certification, every child I tested showed a delay in development within the central nervous system, and most of those same children showed auditory processing problems as well—not hearing problems, but rather, listening difficulties. Fascinating!

As I began working with my own daughter, at the age of 18, stimulating her central nervous system, rapid changes began to take place. Her reading jumped from third-grade level to adult level within 18 months. She started reading books on her own and then shared with me what she had read. She found she was able to read a recipe, follow it and have success in cooking or baking. Her eye movements were suddenly stable, even when she engaged in cognitive processing such as reading, writing or copying. We continued with Neuro-Developmental Delay (NDD) Therapy for the next 18 months.

At a specific point during the NDD Therapy, she began The Listening Fitness Program. Her speech changed overnight, literally! She had never been able to pronounce multi-syllable words. She could manage to articulate the first and last syllables, but she could not articulate words and include middle syllables accurately. If I broke words down for her and had her repeat each word, syllable by syllable, she could do it; but then she could not put all of the syllables together and say the complete word. Then one day after beginning the Listening Fitness Program she said "Tchaikovsky," and I was stunned. I asked her to say it again and offered to buy her a CD. She said it again, and her smile extended from one ear to the other. I hurriedly pulled out a 300-word, high-school level vocabulary book and together we read every single word. I said a word and she repeated each word. She pronounced them all accurately the first time without having to break each word into syllables first. Amazing!

About this time I noticed she was singing with the congregation in church. Previously, she either struggled with reading the words or couldn't keep up with everyone else; therefore, she never sang. Now she sings right along with everyone else, and if I am standing next to her, I can hear her voice. She also started singing in front of the family when choosing to be silly, such as with Veggie Tales songs. She can sing with rhythm and well enough that anyone who did not know her as a child would never guess she had been literally incapable of singing for most of her life.

Soon her personality relaxed and blossomed. She began to understand jokes and laughed with the rest of the family. She began to laugh at herself. She could repeat jokes, and we observed some wit for the first time. I began hearing, "Mom, let me read this comic to you. It's really funny!" Life became enjoyable for her. The angry and belligerent behavior ceased. Looking at who she is now, it's hard to believe the previous behavior had ever been part of her life. Friends began commenting that she was blossoming and maturing, showing eye contact, engaging in conversation, developing a personality. Her eyes began to sparkle and she appeared and behaved like a truly happy young lady, comfortable with her surroundings.

I remember fretting over how she would handle having all of her wisdom teeth pulled at one time. Would she fight the doctor? Would several people have to hold her down in order to administer the anesthetic? Would I once again find myself unable to do anything to alleviate her fear? I stood next to her as they strapped her into the chair. She was not alarmed in the least, even though I was trembling inside. She talked calmly to the doctor and asked for gas before the shot. He gladly acquiesced, and we continued to chat. Soon she became quite talkative and the doctor gave her the shot. The next thing she knew, it was all over and she was fine. Wow! What a difference!

Orientation and spatial awareness developed. One day she told me she was going for a walk in our neighborhood. Outwardly I shrugged it off with "OK, see you later," but inwardly I thought, "You're leaving by *yourself* to take a walk, and you know how to find your way back home? *Wow!*" Another day she invited a friend over for the afternoon, and they decided to take a walk. When they came back she told me they went to a nearby park and played on the swings. Shocked that she could tolerate the movement of a swing, I asked if she actually sat on a swing and swung. She said, "Yeah, it was fun." She surprised me one day when as we entered one of our routine department stores she said, "I'll meet up with you later." Now we always split up in department stores and later meet back at a designated place. I can drop her off at the door to the grocery store and wait for her to go find items without losing her bearings, then purchase them and return to find me waiting in the car.

She knows I find tremendous pleasure in Starbucks drinks. Often when she and I are out running errands together, she asks if we can stop at Starbucks so she can treat me to a drink. What she has not known is the greater pleasure I find in waiting in the car while she goes *by herself* to place the order, pays for it *by herself* and then is *able* to maneuver herself back into the car with the drink and her purse in her hands. I watch ecstatically as she no longer seems to be afraid of the world and has begun to do things independently.

She began to feel pain. It seemed the pendulum had swung in the opposite direction because all of a sudden a simple paper cut was intolerable. Suddenly everything hurt, and the imbalance in regulating the severity of pain became a difficult challenge. This has slowly begun to stabilize and continues to do so. Now she appreciates hugs and affection. She often approaches me with, "I need a mommy hug," or "You look like you could use a hug."

We started noticing a barefoot young lady walking around the house. The socks disappeared, except when appropriate. More fitted clothes became acceptable. She started wearing jeans instead of loose-fitting clothes such as sweatpants. Texture no longer bothers her.

I began observing a teenager in front of a mirror. Whereas she used to refuse to look at herself in a mirror, even to brush her hair, she now spends lots of time in front of the mirror.

She took her first shower at the age of 19. Although she prefers baths to showers, she can and does choose to take showers. It delights me every time I hear the shower running instead of bathwater. She has not become an avid swimmer (although she has gone swimming), but at least she is no longer afraid of water.

One day she asked me to take her to the fabric store. By herself, she chose a pattern, fabric and trims and asked me to make a dress for her. I was surprised that she knew what she wanted and astonished that she could visualize the final product. After I made the dress, she chose shoes to go with it on her own. Her completed outfit is very attractive and draws compliments every time she wears it.

Towards the end of NDD Therapy I noticed changes in her posture and she became more coordinated. Now when she sits or stands, her head is erect and aligned, not resting to one side in a tilted manner. No longer does she curl over at the table and rest her head on an arm. She can do jumping jacks! I remember a girl who never crossed midline, yet now she crosses her legs or ankles, sits cross-legged on the floor, crosses her arms. I find delight in observing her posture in church. Dressed in a skirt and heels, she often crosses one leg over the other at the knee. This is new and exciting to see!

Visualization and verbal expression appeared. She began sharing with me dreams she had the previous night. I never, ever heard about a dream until she was 19 years old. Now she reads stories or watches movies and wants to share the plot with me. I can follow it and understand it and grasp the sequence of events. Sometimes I may not be interested in the story or movie, but then I remind myself that this is coming from a young lady who was literally incapable of such expression until just recently. Let her talk! She'll tell me what she agrees with and disagrees with, likes and dislikes. Just recently she said she thought the author of the fantasy book she was reading had developed a very good story, but she completely disagreed with his general philosophy of life as it was conveyed in the book. Seemingly "out of the blue" she began to express her own thoughts and opinions. Not only has verbal expression exploded, but her written expression is much more creative, more detailed, more interesting.

Spelling and writing improved several grade levels within about two months. I was astounded when I realized I could read her writing and understand what she was trying to communicate. Better sentence development began, and a love for creative writing surfaced. She started writing me notes and letters, expressing her feelings, emotions and thoughts. I remember one letter in particular because it expressed very clearly why she was angry with me. As I read each line, I grew more and more excited. And, as soon as I finished, I ran to her bedroom absolutely beside myself. She looked up at me in puzzlement, and I said, "Look at this *beautiful* letter! There's not one single spelling mistake on this entire piece of paper!" I was ecstatic beyond words.

She began writing children's stories. While I remember a girl who detested writing and could not write legibly no matter how hard she tried, she now often spends several hours a day writing and re-writing stories that are interesting, descriptive, full of expression and dialogue, very creative and definitely imaginative. Following is a short story she wrote based on a word list I gave her from which she was asked to develop a story of her choosing (the underlined words are the words she used to develop the story). What I found so amazing is that before NDD Therapy or the Listening Fitness Program she could never have written this, or any, story. She did not understand sequencing of events, cause-and-effect, wit and humor.

Once upon a time there lived a man and his chestnut horse. The man was said to be involved in witchcraft. He lived in a small cottage on a hilltop. He was old but had high energy for his age.

One day he was sitting at his table eating when his milkman set some milk on his doorstep and ran for it. The old man laughed to himself. His name was Merlin.

Soon he heard a knock on his door.

"Someone is at the door," said his horse. They heard voices.

"I tell you, he's a crackpot," said one voice.

"I heard he's an old nitwit," said another voice.

Merlin set his drumstick down. "Nitwit am I?" he muttered. Merlin opened the door.

"Well, what is it? You must want something to run _uphill_ to my door," said Merlin sharply.

"Well, you see our cat got _kidnapped_ and we thought you had him," said a boy with a squeaky voice.

"I hate cats," said Merlin as his face turned _reddish_ from the light of the setting sun.

"Bobby, you _upset_ the old _dimwit_," said a tall boy.

"Bobby, how about a dog instead?" asked Merlin.

"Boy, would I!" said Bobby excitedly.

"Hoppity, whoppity, boppity," chanted Merlin. The tall boy turned into a _bulldog_. "Now go. Your cat Fluffy got eaten by a wolf," said Merlin.

Bobby skipped off with his new pet.

Fine motor skills seemed to develop out of nowhere. Coordination of fingers fell into place. All of a sudden she could play card games and deal cards rapidly while counting out hands. She is amazingly fast at the game of Speed, a card game that demands rapid hand and finger movements, along with quick mental processing. She told me excitedly one day that she had just successfully counted out hands while dealing cards as her cousin had at the same time called out random numbers in an attempt to distract her and make her lose track of her deal. She recognized she was able to ignore the intended distraction and focus on the task at hand.

Drawing abilities changed phenomenally. Her drawings used to be one-dimensional—flat, like Egyptian hieroglyphics in style. She took private art lessons for nearly two years as a teenager, yet her drawings continually showed no depth, dimension or proportion. After a few months of Neuro-Developmental Delay Therapy, her drawings suddenly took on depth, shading, proportion and tremendous detail. Her ability to draw flowers and animals with good proportion has impressed me.

Age: 13

Age: 16

Age: 21

Age: 21

She began grasping procedures in problem solving and working out math problems mentally. Suddenly she understood when a problem called for addition, or subtraction, or addition then multiplication, and so forth. I saw a difference in something as simple as a game of Yahtzee—she no longer used a calculator to total her score. Her number columns became aligned, and she began adding her score correctly by hand.

She finally grasped judgment of distance and space around her. She began to understand time and the difference in time zones around the world. She began doing her bank deposits and withdrawals independently as well as shopping independently. She enjoys working large, complex tabletop or 3-D puzzles, something she never even attempted before we began the therapy. She demonstrates a curiosity about the world—how things work, which stars make up specific constellations, the flight pattern of our trip on a vacation, the locations of specific cities or countries, world events, politics, sports, movies.

As we continued with NDD Therapy, I became aware of an additional cause for concern. I am convinced that she not only suffered 18 years with a dysfunctional central nervous system and poor auditory processing, but also with an underdeveloped digestive system.

She had always been a picky eater, and by the time she was 16 she was down to about four foods: peanut butter sandwiches, cereal, oatmeal and, of course, chocolate. One summer she became so ill she vomited every time she ate and dropped 15 pounds within a three-week period. I was frightened, as she was already underweight. Doctors ran tests and came up with nothing. All they could offer was a drug to stop the vomiting. I did not want to stop the vomiting; I wanted to know what was wrong. So, once again, I took matters into my own hands.

I started treatment with the assumption that her digestive system was incapable of proper digestion and unable to properly absorb nutrients. Within three days the vomiting stopped. Within a few months she had gained back the weight she lost and then some. Appetite! She began eating constantly, like a teenager should! No longer is she a picky eater who chooses only a few foods. She gladly tries new foods and shows healthy digestion and absorption.

As her digestion began functioning better, I witnessed another shift in her disposition. I saw increased stamina, less lethargy, improved mental alertness and motivation to get physical exercise. Hardly a day goes by now that she does not spend time walking the treadmill, riding the stationary bicycle, or doing floor exercises. I still sense an inner flutter of surprise every time she tells me she's going to the basement to exercise.

She has become friendly, personable, compassionate and easy-going. I would never think of describing her as an angry or belligerent person. When she gets angry, it is no longer based on fear, and she deals with it through reasoning and talking it out.

She does not like to travel; she prefers her own home and personal surroundings. She can easily become anxious or nervous. I used to see a child who responded to uncomfortable situations with complete withdrawal and extreme fear; now I see a person who can change and show flexibility, even in what feels like an uncomfortable situation for her. She might be anxious or nervous, but she can get through whatever it is. She is still shy and easily intimidated by parents who bring their children for therapy. She shared with me that she often wonders if parents are scrutinizing her based on what they have heard about her, and it makes her uncomfortable, as it would anyone.

At the age of 19 she rode a 10-speed bicycle one day when the two of us went on a bike ride. Afterward, she said that although she was able to do it, she prefers a bicycle which has the brakes attached to the pedals instead of the handlebars. But she tried it!

She loves to read, write, draw and study science and history on her own. As a typical parent, I see such wonderful changes that I forget how far we have come and how much she has accomplished. I repeatedly make the mistake of raising the bar. Now that she reads, writes and functions as a whole person, I have found myself saying, "So, when do you plan to start college classes?" She lets me know that right now she is not interested in taking college courses. And I have to realize that she needs time to adjust to who she is. She can relax and enjoy herself, her new interests and her ability to function normally for the first time in her life.

Inexpressible joy overflows my heart when I find her sprawled out in front of the fireplace or curled up in a comfortable chair, deeply engrossed in a several-hundred-page book. Going to the library has become a weekly event. The library workers know her by name and often discuss books and movies with her. Just recently, while running errands, I stopped at the library to get a specific book for her. The book was checked out to someone else. There I was standing in an aisle in the library, talking on my cell phone with my daughter, reading off names of books by two of her favorite authors—something I never imagined I would do for her. I continually heard, "Nope, I read that one." Finally I found one she had not read. It was wonderful! These were 400-page books! She also loves listening to books on tape, something she could never have done just four years ago. She could not have maintained focus or visualized the story as it was told.

My daughter is currently undergoing treatment by a chiropractor for scoliosis. Although she had routine chiropractic care from the time she was six years old, I started to notice peculiar standing posture and an abnormal gait when she was about 14. I habitually told her, "Stand up straight." She would shift her torso around a bit, but never straighten up. I wondered about it but attributed it to another of her several peculiarities. Friends and relatives suggested I take her to an orthopedist, but I wasn't ready to take any steps. My instincts told me we had deeper issues to face first.

Further education and appropriate timing for treatment came together just recently. As an NDD therapist I regularly attend international conferences sponsored by The Institute for Neuro-Physiological Psychology. Most recently I attended a conference in Pisa, Italy, where Professor Alain Berthoz, a neurophysiologist and professor at Collège de France, was one of the featured speakers. In his presentation he discussed the vestibular system and its association with scoliosis. Bells went off in my head, and I came home with his comments burning in my brain. Some quick research showed me that chiropractors are aware of this connection. And I suddenly realized what had most likely happened with my daughter: if the vestibular system is highly dysfunctional, the body is incapable of sensing straightness or vertical alignment. How would the spine "know" to grow vertically straight without the vestibular system telling it what straight is? I guessed that my daughter showed peculiar posture and an odd gait at the age of 14, after years of regular chiropractic care, because during the age of rapid growth her vestibular system had not been functioning properly.

Just recently I took her to a chiropractor and shared with him her history. An initial exam and x-rays showed 17-degree left lumbar scoliosis (lateral curve) and a 6-mm pelvic deficiency on the left side. The chiropractor gave her a lift to wear in her left shoe, and she began chiropractic treatments the following week. Although it's too soon to notice possible changes or results, I have observed reactions and responses in my daughter that I never saw from previous chiropractic treatments. In all her early years of routine chiropractic care my daughter never showed outward signs of the central nervous system being aware of or responding to chiropractic treatment. This time I observed signs of response and awareness in the central nervous system in her first week of treatment. Sleeping patterns changed immediately. Her immune system was affected right away as she became ill the day after her first treatment. She needed an afternoon nap every day for the first week. Initially she felt and showed signs of fatigue, and her joints were tender. After her second treatment she said, "All those times you told me to stand up straight I didn't know what you meant. I thought I was straight." For the first time in her life she became internally aware that her spine is not straight.

I see value in treating the vestibular system prior to treating scoliosis. I shared with our chiropractor that I believe her vestibular system needed to be treated first and, now that her vestibular system has matured, she is ready for chiropractic treatment of the scoliosis. He agreed. I have since discussed this order of treatment with a cranio-sacral therapist. Her immediate response was, "That makes sense!"

Time will tell for my daughter regarding successful treatment of her scoliosis. In the meantime, all this has made me wonder if it is possible to prevent certain cases of scoliosis in children by treating them Neuro-Developmentally before they reach the age of rapid growth.

A beautiful young lady, my daughter plans to be a children's storybook writer, a goal that would never have surfaced prior to the discoveries we made and the advances she has experienced. When she's not spending two hours every day writing, she works as my assistant, helping other children and adults who also have NDD, auditory processing and listening difficulties, digestive dysfunction and/or academic struggles.

I found myself teary-eyed and emotional as I wrote this story, for it resurfaced many memories, heartaches and struggles. Yet, I can easily begin sobbing over who my daughter has become; I am so incredibly grateful for the answers we have found.

Do most of the people I see have all of the struggles my daughter experienced? No; but they often relate to several of them to some degree. Typically I find signs of neurological dysfunction that originate in the brain stem and vary in levels of severity from person to person. Many times I also find listening difficulties that manifest themselves as sound sensitivity, attention and/or discrimination difficulties, again in varying degrees of severity. Occasionally I'll see only one of the two. In other cases I also see signs of digestive dysfunction. It is quite rare to find academics unaffected. But difficulties in academics typically are not the foundational problem. For many children, the root of the problem is three-fold: Neuro-Developmental Delay, auditory processing and listening, and digestive or immune dysfunction.

My daughter became a whole person through Neuro-Developmental Delay Therapy and the Listening Fitness Program. I eagerly and excitedly watch other children become whole individuals through these two therapies as well. Most parents ask me, "What is NDD Therapy, and how does it differ from the numerous intervention programs available?" The next chapter addresses these questions.

Early Development and its Influence on Behavior and Learning

An initial Neuro-Developmental Delay (NDD) assessment determines the overall functioning of an individual's central nervous system. It includes standard medical, neurological, psychological, oculo-motor and visual-perceptual tests as well as an assessment of listening skills. Parents observe the entire assessment and are able to see first-hand their child's specific physiological dysfunctions. In the majority of children I see, the root problem stems from one or more stages of early development.

As a baby develops inside his mother's womb, his central nervous system develops from the bottom up. In other words, the first movements are generated from the spinal cord, followed by spontaneous or involuntary movements from the brain stem. Within several months following birth, controlled movements are generated from the midbrain and the cerebellum. Later, reasoning and processing develop from the cortex. The brain develops from the spinal cord to the brain stem and then to the upper levels of the brain. Yet, when behavior or academic problems surface, specialists tend to deal with the problems from the top down. They often attempt to deal with the difficulties in the reverse order of development. When learning problems are first detected, the tendency is to start testing the functioning of the cortex, and when motor or sensory problems appear, specialists tend to pursue various stimulations of the midbrain. Treatment should begin, however, with the source of the problem.

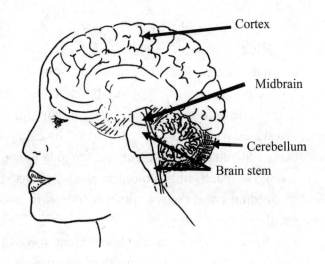

I have found that I have greater success in helping individuals overcome their presenting difficulties by first determining the initial point of breakdown or dysfunction, then treating the problem(s) from that point of development upward—from the initial point of developmental dysfunction to the upper regions of the brain. One mother told me that educational psychologists determined her son was in need of occupational, sensory integration, vision and auditory processing therapies. Her response to the psychologists, and the research that led her to my work, was an insightful observation that collectively these areas of difficulties for her son must be an indication that her child has neurological dysfunction. Many of the children in my practice have already undergone therapies such as those listed above, with minimal, if any, success. For these children, dysfunction begins in the brain stem. Therefore, it is necessary to treat the brain stem first.

The brain stem

The brain stem is multi-functioning. Primitive reflexes are mediated in the brain stem, gross motor pathways cross at the brain stem level and vestibular messages pass through the brain stem. Interestingly, all the cranial nerves, except the olfactory and optic nerves, originate in the brain stem. This includes the oculo-motor nerve, which is directly related to eye movements.

The brain stem is the foundation of movement for a child from birth to four months of age. These movements are spontaneous and reflexive; they are involuntary responses and do not require cortical control. And "it is the[se] primitive reflexes which lay the foundation for all later functioning".[1] A baby uses these reflexes in the womb, as well as during the birth process as it works its way through the birth canal. Normal birth delivery helps the baby strengthen these reflexes. After birth they function to provide for automatic survival, such as feeding or lying on the tummy and turning the head to allow for continued breathing. Physicians regularly check for these reflexes during well-baby exams.

It is more than likely that certain reflexes are crucial for survival in the first months of life and that under-developed Moro and Asymmetrical Tonic Neck reflexes may be a factor in Sudden Infant Death Syndrome (SIDS) – the Moro reflex because it should provide an instant arousal mechanism and the ATNR because it should prevent the baby from lying face down when placed on its tummy.[2]

Between the ages of four months and one year these primitive reflexes should inhibit or withdraw. A mature brain functions from the cortex down, so that the rest of the brain responds to the orders given by the cortex.

But what might occur if the primitive reflexes in the brain stem do not inhibit or withdraw as they should in normal development? Helen Bee in *The Developing Child* says about these primitive reflexes, "If present *past* this age [about six months old], however, such a rudimentary reflex may be a sign of some neurological difficulty".[3] For more than 30 years, The Institute for Neuro-Physiological Psychology (INPP) has been directly involved in research to determine the effects of aberrant reflexes on behavior and academic learning. INPP is also involved in training therapists in this discipline. Their work and training is the cornerstone of my practice.

Primitive Reflexes

The primitive reflex called the Moro reflex is a startle reflex. It can be initiated by a sudden reaction to stimuli or loss of head support.

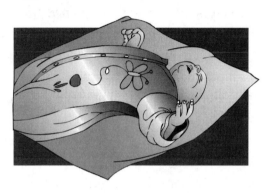

[The] arms and legs will open out from the characteristic flexed posture of the new-born, there will be a rapid intake of breath, and the baby will "freeze" in that position for a fraction of a second, before the arms and legs return across the body, usually accompanied by a cry of protest.[4]

"[T]he Moro reflex could help the baby move away from unpleasant things".[5] It "is an involuntary response to threat".[6] If a child is still functioning with a Moro reflex response long after the reflex should have inhibited, he or she may demonstrate a "fight or flight" reaction—act first, think later. The Moro reflex activates the limbic and hormonal systems, which means it significantly affects emotions. Individuals with a retained Moro reflex may demonstrate over-reactive, over-sensitive or over-excited behaviors, poor impulse control and/or the inability to modulate and regulate responses in given situations.

I see many children with a retained Moro reflex, and they usually demonstrate highly emotional behavior such as aggression, argumentativeness, anger, over-sensitivity or extreme withdrawal. They typically react—instead of respond—to people and circumstances based on their immediate emotional status. They often have known or hidden digestive disorders, poorly developed immune systems (many have or show signs of yeast overgrowth) or unusual sensitivities (overly sensitive or under-sensitive) to one or more sensory stimuli (smell, light, sound, taste, texture, touch). Some children experience tactile sensitivities (over- or under-sensitive) in specific areas such as the hands, the face or the scalp. They may describe themselves as "super ticklish"; others feel no sense of touch.

It is exciting to watch such behaviors diminish as the Moro reflex inhibits through INPP's Neuro-Developmental Delay (NDD) Therapy. If a child no longer suffers from significant reactive impulses, he is better able to cope with a classroom environment and focus on academics without distractions. Typically this child then becomes more aware of and more interested in the world around him; he no longer manifests fear-based or anger-based behavior. Actions become significantly less emotionally based. Many children show some degree of change in the functioning of their immune system and/or digestive system. Allergies may be less severe, or disappear altogether. The immune system may seem weaker at first and then stronger as the child progresses through NDD Therapy. Eating habits often change, and I hear parents say quite frequently that their children are willing to try new foods more than ever before. Hyper or hypo tactile sensitivity reduces or diminishes, along with unusual sensitivities to light and/or sound.

The Asymmetric Tonic Neck Reflex (ATNR) begins in the womb and may be noticed when the pregnant mother feels kicking. This reflex, in the womb, stimulates the balance mechanism and helps the fetus to develop muscle tone. It "increases neural connections ... The ATNR not only assists the birth process but is reinforced by it".[7]

This reflex can be observed in a newborn by turning her head to one side. The arm and leg on the same side extend and the arm and leg on the opposite side bend. Where the head goes, the arm and eyes go. This is significant to an older child trying to learn to write. If the arm and eyes are still following the movement of the head, problems arise with writing, copying, posture or eye tracking in reading. Children with a retained ATNR are often the children with dyslexic tendencies. Writing becomes very difficult, eye tracking is usually not fully developed, and the ability to think and write at the same time can be affected. Although the child can think of ideas, he struggles with putting his ideas on paper. Multi-tasking becomes quite difficult. Posture is affected. I have seen teenagers sit in an ATNR position. One knee is up with the foot on the seat of the chair, while the arm on the same side of the body is bent at the elbow; the other leg extends straight out from the chair, and the arm on the same side is extended; and the head faces toward the extended arm. A 13-year-old girl told me that such a position was the most comfortable way for her to sit even though it annoyed her mother, especially at the dinner table. Individuals I have seen in my practice that have language, copying or writing difficulties of any kind have *all* shown evidence to some extent of an ATNR. Most of them also struggle with discerning their right from their left.

As these children begin to inhibit the ATNR, they also begin to exhibit better handwriting, written expression, hand-eye tracking and innate awareness of their own right and left. Parents often share with me that their children not only show improved academic skills, but also better form in their various physical activities, whether it be roller skating, running while playing, karate class, gymnastics, soccer or baseball.

Rooting, sucking and swallowing reflexes all allow for good feeding in a newborn. The Rooting reflex can be initiated by touching an infant's face on either side of the mouth. The head turns and the mouth opens in readiness for sucking.

But, when retained, these oral reflexes "will result in continued sensitivity and immature responses to touch in the mouth region—particularly in the area of the lip".[8] An older child who still manifests these reflexes will often show hypersensitivity around the lips and mouth. Chewing may be difficult, especially with certain foods, and speech and articulation may be affected.

The Palmar and Plantar reflexes are manifested in the hands and feet. If a finger or other object is placed in the infant's hand, the baby grasps the finger or object firmly.

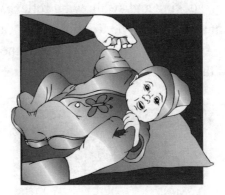

"The Plantar reflex is a similar but weaker response in the feet to pressure being applied to the base of the toes."[9]

A continuation of the Palmar reflex in the older child can affect pencil grip, independent thumb movement, speech and palm sensitivity. A retained Plantar reflex can be observed through poor standing and walking stability and is sometimes the "toe walker." Having observed children as they work through these reflexes, I have seen them independently correct their pencil grip, show less or no sensitivity in the palms and go from being toe walkers to feet walkers. One boy in particular showed significant improvement in balance during his karate class at about the same time my tests indicated inhibition of his Plantar and other primitive reflexes.

The Tonic Labyrinthine reflex (TLR) is closely related to the Moro reflex in the first few months of life, as both reflexes are activated by movement of the head. When an adult lays a baby across her arm and tucks the baby's head forward, the baby goes into a fetal position.

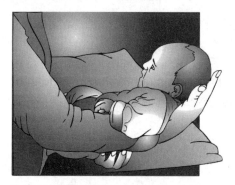

When the baby's head falls below spine level, the body pushes up and out so that the torso extends as well.

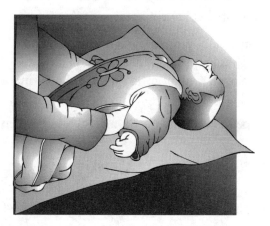

The TLR "exerts a tonic influence upon the distribution of muscle tone throughout the body literally helping the neonate to 'straighten out' from the flexed posture of the fetus and the newborn".[10] An older child who manifests a retained or residual TLR is sometimes called the "floppy child," or she might demonstrate the opposite—excessive body rigidity. This reflex can interfere in learning to creep on the hands and knees. Retention of the TLR can throw off one's center of balance and affect eye movements. Such individuals often struggle with judging space, distance, orientation, and depth. They typically have poor eye convergence, which is necessary for reading.

As children in my practice begin to inhibit this reflex and eye convergence stabilizes, their teachers have frequently contacted the parents to share and discuss improvements in reading. Many parents have been quite astounded at their child's sudden interest in reading. Posture and balance also improve, and parents easily notice this in their child's karate moves, gymnastics, bike riding or soccer.

The Spinal Galant reflex appears to be involved during the birth process as it allows small rotational movements of the baby's pelvis on either side as it works its way down the birth canal.

Stimulation of the skin on either side of the spine in the lumbar region causes flexion of the hip on the side that has been stimulated and arching of the remainder of the body in the opposite direction in an avoidance reaction.[11]

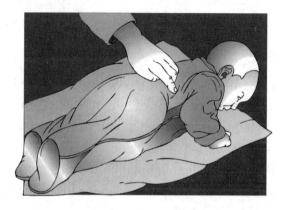

It has also been suggested that this reflex may conduct sound **in utero** as it vibrates up through the body. I have found in my practice that nearly all of the children who initially manifested a retained Spinal Galant reflex no longer showed the reflex after they completed the Listening Fitness Program (another foundation stone of my practice). Symptoms of a retained Spinal Galant reflex might be fidgetiness, bedwetting beyond the age of five, poor short-term memory and poor concentration. These children might be the ones described as "ants-in-the-pants" children. Dr. Beuret, "working with adults in Chicago, found the Spinal Galant reflex to be present in a high percentage of patients suffering from Irritable Bowel Syndrome".[12] In my own practice I have seen symptoms of digestive disorders in many children who also have retention of multiple primitive reflexes. Interestingly, some children suffer with bedwetting yet do not have a Spinal Galant reflex. I have found bedwetting to be related to vestibular dysfunction, as most of these children stop bedwetting either through the Listening Fitness Program or some other form of vestibular stimulation.

The Symmetric Tonic Neck Reflex (STNR) appears between six and nine months of age, remains for two or three months and then withdraws. This reflex causes an infant to position himself on his hands and knees in preparation for creeping and eventually walking. The head goes back, the upper half of the body straightens and the lower half bends.

When the head goes down, the upper half of the body goes with it and the legs begin to extend. A study in 1988 found that "many cognitive skills, such as object permanence and space perception, are learned during the creeping period—and not until then".[13] If the STNR is retained, it can affect integration between the upper and lower sections of the body—they don't want to work together. It may also affect posture when sitting. Such children may slump when sitting in a chair, sit in a "w" leg position on the floor with the knees together and each leg turned outward, move in a clumsy manner and struggle with vertical hand-eye coordination:

> The focusing distance and hand-eye coordination skills used in the act of creeping are at the same distance that the child will eventually use for reading and writing. It has been observed (Pavlides 1987) that a high percentage of children with reading difficulties omitted the stages of crawling and creeping in infancy.[14]

I have found it significant that nearly 100 percent of the individuals I have tested have shown evidence to some degree of an STNR. While tutoring these children in academics, I do not ask them to sit in chairs at a table or desk until this reflex is nearly fully inhibited. They are much more comfortable and productive in their own postural positions. As I observe the reflex begin the process of inhibition, the child's posture changes and he or she eventually moves to a chair at a desk. Copying information typically improves dramatically at this point, as the eyes are now able to accommodate near-to-far-to-near for copying from papers, books or chalkboards.

Following are typical sitting positions of an older child with retained primitive reflexes. When one or more of the TLR, ATNR or STNR is retained, the child's head, eyes and body often do not automatically move independently, especially when cognitive skills are engaged. As the head turns, so go the eyes, arms and sometimes the torso. "Head control is an essential prerequisite for the development of all later functions and should be the prime initiator of early movement, tonus and balance."[15] Yet I often see children who exert very poor head or eye control. Arms and legs tend to maintain similar positions to those of their earlier developmental stages. Parents and teachers find themselves repeatedly saying, "Sit up straight," to no avail.

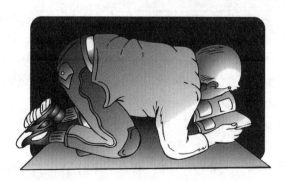

The vestibular system

Because vestibular messages pass through the brain stem, it is not unusual to find vestibular dysfunction when brain stem reflexes show dysfunction. The vestibular system directs our balance and equilibrium, and its transmissions are critical to early brain development:

> A mature vestibular system is what allows the fetus to sense his own orientation with respect to gravity and to turn into the proper position (head down) in the weeks or days before birth. Indeed, babies born with defects in their vestibular system have a much greater chance of being in a breech position, presumably because they can't adequately discern the difference between up and down.[16]

A mature vestibular system consists of more than just being able to automatically balance ourselves in various bodily positions. It also plays an essential role in accurate eye movements. Researchers often evaluate the status of a developing vestibular system by observing eye gaze.[17] Listening and auditory skills are affected by balance as well. The vestibular system begins its development in the inner ear. It separates into its own system in early development and matures at a much faster rate than the sense of hearing. Certain drugs which are known to cause deafness can also cause permanent vestibular dysfunction.[18]

Typically, I find that children with brain stem dysfunction also have vestibular dysfunction in motor movements, eye movements and/or auditory processing. In my practice many children are unable to maintain balance when standing with the feet together. Other children are unable to keep their balance when standing on one foot, which has been associated with language disabilities. Some children cannot balance when standing with one foot in front of the other, heel-to-toe, as if on a balance beam. Many children in my practice cannot maintain balance unless the body is in motion. Eye gaze is dependent on good vestibular functioning, and without exception I have found poor eye movements in varying degrees of severity when I test these children. Good auditory functioning is also dependent on good vestibular functioning. A large percentage of the children I test show auditory dysfunction in varying levels of severity. As these children experience NDD Therapy, they begin to show better balance—standing on one foot, riding a bicycle for the first time, improved control of body movements, better orientation and body awareness, as well as stabilized eye movements and better auditory processing.

Motor pathways

Motor pathways cross in the brain stem. The left hemisphere controls body movements on the right side, and the right hemisphere controls body movements on the left side. These pathways cross to opposite sides of the body in the brain stem. Therefore, it is not unusual to find motor movement difficulties when brain stem dysfunction exists. Some children do not have a dominant hand, foot, eye or ear. Some only use one side of their body. Some use the right and left sides in mirror movements—whatever one arm does, the other does precisely the same. Many of these children seem awkward in gross and/or fine motor movements. Some walk, run, march, roller skate and so forth in homolateral patterns— the arm extends with the leg on the same side of the body instead of with the opposite leg. Parents often share with me, at specific times during NDD Therapy, that they have unexpectedly noticed a change in their child's motor movements. Seemingly overnight, they see their children run, skate or swim in natural cross-pattern movements.

The midbrain and postural reflexes

As the primitive reflexes in the brain stem inhibit, new reflexes should begin to emerge. These are called postural reflexes because they involve movements for crawling, creeping and walking—postural. Postural reflexes should be present by three-and-a-half years of age, and we should retain these reflexes for life. They are initiated from the midbrain and gradually override involuntary movements of the brain stem. Many treatment programs provide therapy from the perspective of initiating stronger midbrain and cerebellum control, thereby superseding involuntary movements of the brain stem. I am finding, however, that for many individuals, brain stem reflexes are still dominant after these treatments and are hindering the proper functioning of the midbrain and cerebellum, regardless of the amount of stimulation:

> If the primitive reflexes are still strong, however, stimulation of postural reflexes alone will rarely reap concomitant changes in the areas of fine muscle coordination, oculomotor functioning,

perceptual processing and academic performance. This may be because, while motor training programs strengthen postural control, they fail to inhibit those retained primitive reflexes which continue to impede the processing of information in the brain.[19]

Once the primitive reflexes are inhibited and the postural reflexes begin to emerge, parents usually observe improved posture when sitting, standing and walking. Academic abilities begin to come together more completely. Observance of vestibular changes, reflex changes and auditory processing changes takes place; the entire process is one of systematic developmental progression, in the same order that development should have naturally occurred.

Anna's House therapy program

My therapy program is typically threefold: Neuro-Developmental Delay (NDD) Therapy, a Listening Fitness Program and academic tutoring. Children in my practice need NDD Therapy so that the brain stem becomes submissive to the higher centers of the brain. Through NDD Therapy, which consists of precise, non-invasive physical movements ("exercises"), I have seen many children begin to function without involuntary movements from the brain stem; the midbrain and cerebellum begin to function as they should, with minimal or no stimulation, and then the cortex takes control. For many children in my practice, the postural reflexes usually begin to emerge on their own as the primitive reflexes withdraw. Other children need minor stimulation.

The Listening Fitness Program is the most ideal sound therapy program I have encountered because it is developmental in its approach. I believe this developmental approach is the critical factor in its success with children who have neurological dysfunction. During initial testing, children often exhibit or express their own listening or auditory processing difficulties. Children as young as five, and up through the age of 14, have said, "But I can't listen without my eyes." These children rely on sight in order to determine the accuracy of what they hear. Other children quickly show an inability to sit still when listening and/or when speaking. Many children can follow directions if the directions are simple and only given one at a time. Often, directions are easier to follow if they do not require a response that includes visual processing. For example, a child may be able to follow specific directions that require an oral response or a specific physical activity, but he or she may be unable to complete a worksheet while spoken directions are given (looking at and processing visual stimulus on a worksheet while listening to oral instructions).

Quite often, children who complete the Listening Fitness Program are able to share differences they have experienced such as, "I can pay attention better." "I can get my work done faster without getting distracted." "I can remember directions."

Many children demonstrate an inability to discriminate between certain letter sounds in words—they often hear the correct sounds at the beginning of words but cannot hear the same sounds in the middle or often at the end of words. They may struggle with hearing or discriminating middle syllables. My own daughter said, "I never knew until now [after the Listening Fitness Program] the difference in sound between the words 'soldier' and 'shoulder.'" Another teenager said, "I just realized [after the Listening Fitness Program] the sound difference between 'medley' and 'melody.'" An 11-year-old girl who had been diagnosed with Perceptual Communication Disorder and demonstrated a significant inability to write legibly completed NDD Therapy, a Listening Fitness Program and academic tutoring. She said one day shortly before she graduated, "I never knew there were so many words I had not heard correctly."

NDD Therapy and the Listening Fitness Program together have advanced these children developmentally; and, as a result, behavior and academics have blossomed and shown phenomenal progress. In my practice, a complete NDD Therapy program typically coincides with a Listening Fitness Program. All of the children in my practice start out with NDD Therapy, which stimulates inhibition of the primitive reflexes. Most of them also need a Listening Fitness Program, which begins when NDD re-testing shows they are developmentally ready. It might take one month, three months, or six months—whenever their individual bodies determine readiness.

And they continue their NDD Therapy while completing the Listening Fitness Program. I have been amazed at the changes I have observed through incorporating the listening therapy at the right time in a child's course of treatment. Children begin to hear specific sounds in words;

they can differentiate between beginning, middle and ending sounds; they begin to hear multiple syllables in words; comprehension, oral reading and spelling improve; speech engages or becomes clearer; the ability to follow multiple directions begins; focusing and staying on task improves. I have seen many parents examine their own child's writing with gaping mouths, astounded at the accuracy in spelling and neatness in writing.

Some children need specific academic tutoring in reading, spelling and writing. I have written a curriculum that fills this need. It allows children to incorporate their new listening skills and apply them to academics. Children who complete the curriculum typically advance to above grade level in reading, writing and spelling in a relatively short period of time.

Just as physiological development is orderly, so is cognitive development. Children who have experienced neurological dysfunction are typically behind in one or more academic subjects. As they complete NDD Therapy and a Listening Fitness Program, if needed, choice of curriculum becomes critical. Most curriculums are not designed to be used remedially, nor are they specifically based on developmental growth. A follow-up reading, spelling or writing curriculum to the Listening Fitness Program must be thoroughly immersed in the use of sounds. Many of these children must then be taught how to apply listening to academic learning. Although they have the ability to listen and process sounds correctly, most also need training in how to purposely apply auditory processing, particularly as it applies to reading and spelling. Otherwise they characteristically revert to previous habits (such as using only the visual system).

The final stage in a child's remediation program typically involves completing NDD Therapy and either implementing my own reading/spelling/writing curriculum or tutoring in specific subjects to pull the academics together and bring the child to grade level. Other children need to fuse visual and auditory processing so that the two work concomitantly, instead of allowing the visual system to override or ignore auditory processing. The change-over from the visual to auditory system and then integration of the two together is often observable. As a child begins to merge visual and auditory processing, I am able to detect signs of right-left brain integration. More advanced reasoning skills are observed. I begin to see advancements in grammar, syntax and organized writing. I also notice better math skills, particularly comprehension and implementation of new abilities for problem solving. Spelling significantly improves because the child can now trust what he or she hears in a word and is able to recognize the various phonemes rather than rely solely on the visual system to remember and repeat the correct order of the letters in a specific word. Parents report that their children are finally able to do homework independently and in a timely manner.

Once a child's brain stem dysfunction has been remediated, the midbrain and cerebellum many times begin to initiate more mature functioning. I see a domino effect in reverse. The brain stem shows stability, and the midbrain and cerebellum seem to naturally follow suit. As the brain stem's primitive reflexes inhibit, the postural reflexes often begin to emerge on their own. As the listening skills are enhanced through the Listening Fitness Program, I begin to see auditory processing engage, and, within months, cognitive skills jump significantly and begin to match cognitive abilities. I have seen children who once struggled with basic physical movements and academic concepts become fully functioning, active, academically successful children. Interestingly, parents tend to forget where their child was initially, and I begin to hear things like, "Now, can you make him want to clean his room?" or "How can she get an 'A' in math?" The difficulties are no longer extreme. They have become ordinary child-like behaviors that all parents face every day.

Nicole

*Previous experience with occupational therapy
and vision therapy*

Nicole received occupational therapy between the ages
of three and five, ending before kindergarten when her motor
skills were found to be "within normal ranges for her age."
She spent six months in vision therapy at the age of three. Her
mother shared the following:

> My husband and I thought we had produced the
> perfect child. From infancy through today, [Nicole] has
> always been a happy, delightful child. She doesn't
> have a shy bone in her body. As an infant, [Nicole]
> was content in anyone's arms. As a toddler, she would
> climb into any available lap and win over strangers
> with her captivating smile. Even her quirks were cute.
> Her horrified expression if she touched dirt or mud was
> priceless. She spent her first beach vacation at 18
> months old smack in the middle of a blanket, refusing
> to move any closer to the sand. We thought she was a
> bit of a klutz because she tripped and fell down
> frequently, but we figured that all young kids probably
> did that. I bought a book of week-by-week
> developmental exercises when she was about a year

old, then promptly tossed it as an obviously worthless publication when [Nicole] was unable to do the exercises recommended for her age.

[Nicole]'s first contact with professional daycare providers occurred soon after her third birthday. Two weeks after starting at the daycare center, the center director asked me for permission to test [Nicole]'s motor skills, which the director felt were delayed. I laughed out loud at the suggestion that my daughter was anything less than perfect, but, of course, gave my permission for testing. Lo and behold, [Nicole] was found to be significantly behind in gross and fine motor skills. Occupational therapy began immediately. Vision therapy followed soon after, when the occupational therapist suggested that the source of [Nicole]'s motor problems was visual. The first round of vision therapy lasted six months, but I was warned that she would need more vision therapy in early elementary school.

Nicole began vision therapy again at age eight, and was continuing with what became nearly two years in her second round when I met her—towards the end of third grade. Although her reading was at grade level, her writing skills, according to school testing, were at grade 2.1, nearly two years behind. Her writing showed creativity, but punctuation was often omitted, and sentences were usually extensive run-ons. She had difficulty expressing her thoughts verbally as well as in writing.

Nicole's most glaring academic trouble spot was math, where she was well below grade level. She struggled in all areas of math and often confused place value and basic addition and subtraction, as in the following example:

She attempted to solve the problem by writing it in reverse order: 11-20; then she subtracted correctly in the ones column. But in the tens column, she subtracted the smaller digit from the larger digit— reverse order.

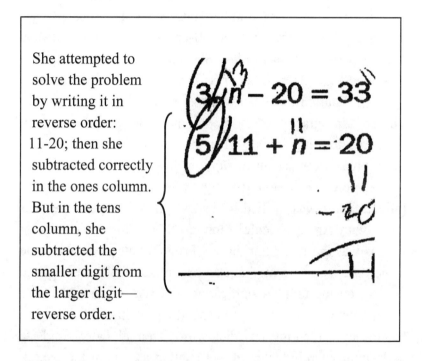

Nicole struggled with more than just academics. She showed extremely poor balance and gross muscle coordination. She was unable to stand with one foot directly in front of the other without falling over. She had a poor sense of rhythm (she was unable to imitate the most basic drum pattern in her Kindermusic class). She also struggled significantly with spatial awareness, body awareness, orientation, occasional bedwetting, hand-eye tracking, visual-motor integration, visual-spatial skills, visual discrimination and auditory skills. Testing showed nearly full retention of all of the primitive reflexes, as well as completely underdeveloped postural reflexes. Her mother observed that "despite her struggles, she had tremendous self-confidence and was always willing to try new activities. She enjoyed participating and was unconcerned that others performed better than she did."

I started a Neuro-Developmental Delay (NDD) Therapy program with Nicole and suggested minimal academic tutoring initially. Her parents had decided to give her a break from vision therapy, at least for the present. Her mother felt that vision therapy "was a grueling ordeal for [Nicole], so I was thrilled to discover that [Nicole] loved her visits with Anna. [Nicole] thought NDD Therapy was great fun, as was the Listening Fitness Program later." At about the same time, Nicole's mother had her treated for Thrush (white coating on the tongue—indicative of yeast overgrowth) by a nutritionist who recommended specific probiotics. Nicole also began supplementing her diet with Essential Fatty Acids, a daily multivitamin, calcium and lecithin as part of the overall plan to achieve optimum brain and neural health.

After three months of NDD Therapy, when I observed improved balance and some inhibition of the Moro and Tonic Neck reflexes, I started Nicole on a 60-hour Listening Fitness Program while continuing NDD Therapy. I restructured the math curriculum so that it paralleled her developmental growth and then tutored her accordingly.

During this time I observed a variety of changes: she became more focused and was able to stay on task, began tying her shoes by herself, completing math drills within the allotted time, and learning the multiplication tables. Her mother observed more mature behavior. Here are three different notes from her mother the following fall (fourth grade):

[Nicole]'s teacher's comment in this week's Monday folder was "Great math thinking with graphs and great participation." I'm still amazed at how far she has come since the end of the last school year. I was in the classroom today. [Nicole] was called on to offer a strategy for solving word problems. She said "make it into a math sentence." About two thirds of the class had to re-take a math facts quiz that she passed the first time.

She brought home a math page today that I will mail to you. I'm pretty sure that this page would have been nearly impossible for her a few months ago. Today, she tossed it aside nonchalantly—no big deal! … Not only was the math easy, but the conversion of a color to a number and back again was no problem! Wow!

I helped out in the classroom today. I actually just sat and listened for 45 minutes of my hour in [Nicole]'s classroom as the teacher walked the class through graphing the height and arm span data that we gathered last week. I was thrilled to see that [Nicole]'s hand was up to answer virtually every question that the teacher asked. She was only called on once, and her answer was correct. She was definitely engaged in the activity. No daydreaming or spacing out that we used to see when she didn't understand the topic ... I asked if [Nicole] has any trouble with distraction or appearing lost and the teacher said "absolutely not." She said [Nicole] is very focused throughout the day.

Following Nicole's 60-hour Listening Fitness Program, I gave her daily auditory maintenance exercises and continued NDD Therapy. Six months later, I added an additional 20-hour listening Boost. The Spinal Galant reflex then tested as completely inhibited and occasional bedwetting ceased. Her oral reading improved phenomenally. She had begun listening to her own voice as she read, and therefore, the reading speed slowed down, she paused between sentences and added inflection. I continued NDD Therapy and tutoring in math, and started coaching her in writing skills. She later began violin lessons at school. Her progress report said she showed outstanding rhythm.

According to her report card, Nicole began fourth grade with writing skills at 2.1 grade level and ended the year at 5.1 grade level—a three-year growth in only one school term! She no longer showed vestibular dysfunction, her gross motor movements were very good and all of the primitive reflexes tested as either completely inhibited or with less than 25 percent evidence. I continued NDD Therapy so as to stimulate the postural reflexes, and tutored three one-hour sessions per week in auditory and visual integration. In the fall of fifth grade, her mother shared the following:

> I asked the music teacher about honor choir. It is open only to fourth and fifth graders. [Nicole] auditioned last year, but didn't make it … The kids had to sight read, sing specific notes, and echo song patterns played on the piano. The music teacher said that [Nicole]'s audition was very strong. She said she was definitely one of the top choices. Each school could only choose seven kids to form the district-wide honor choir! I had no idea she was such a good singer!

Following are some of Nicole's drawings six months after starting an NDD program. The first three were drawn at the age of 9.11, when Nicole was in fourth grade.

Notice the incorrect shape of the diamond and the missing center point in the union jack.

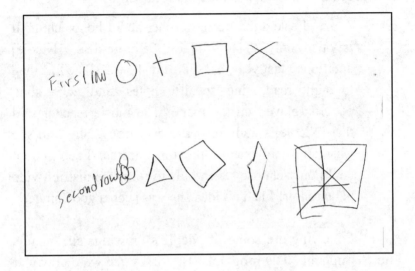

Notice the separated heads, missing arms, enlarged eyes and rounded feet.

Notice the arrangement of the shapes in comparison to the similar example on page 69.

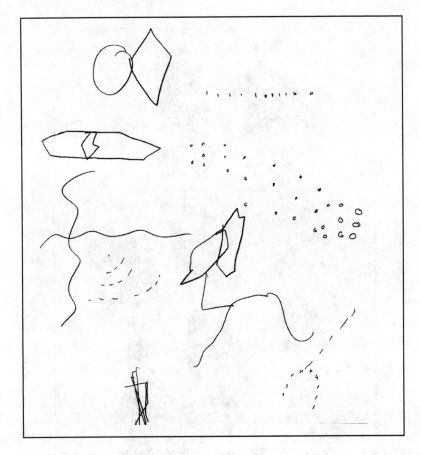

Six months later Nicole was asked to draw the same examples as initially. Indicators of increased body awareness and improved oculo-motor and visual-perceptual skills were evident.

Notice better visual spacing, nicely drawn shapes and the center of the union jack in comparison to the previous drawing.

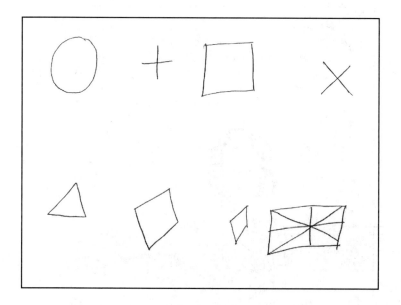

Notice all the body parts are included, the eyes are proportionate, the hands and feet have detail.

Notice nice placement of the shapes, better pencil control, more accurate copying.

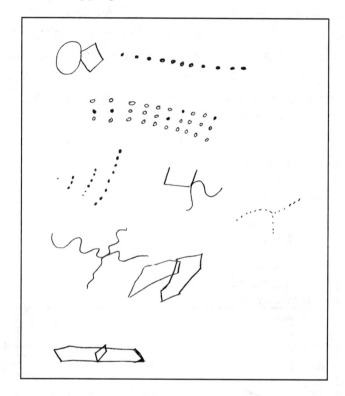

At about this same time, Nicole visited her optometrist for her annual exam—approximately one year after setting aside vision therapy and starting NDD Therapy. Her tracking showed "full and unrestricted motilities," and her focusing showed that she could "maintain near vision objects...for sustained periods of time." My testing showed the same results—remarkable eye-movement improvements from NDD Therapy.

When Nicole began her fifth-grade school year, she received a standardized test progress report that graphed her math skills. Significant growth had occurred during each summer for the past two years. The first summer showed significant growth (#1 on the graph below). That was the summer in which she completed her first 60 hours of the Listening Fitness Program and math tutoring. The second summer (#2 on the graph below) showed phenomenal growth. During that summer I tutored her in math and writing, while continuing with NDD Therapy.

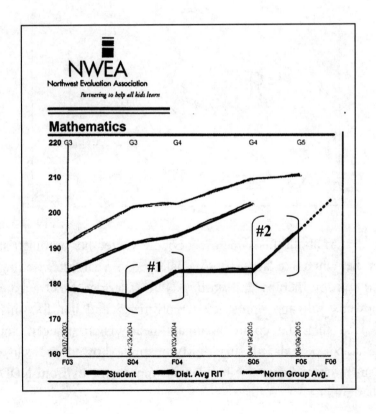

I started observing right-left brain integration regarding Nicole's math and writing skills, and she began to apply advanced reasoning skills. As a fifth grader, Nicole earned first place in an essay-writing contest. Her ending-year report card showed that her writing skills had advanced from 5.1 grade level at the beginning of the school year to 7.1 at the end of the year.

In sixth grade, her first year in middle school, Nicole had completed NDD Therapy, and my only involvement was tutoring math. Her mother and I both noticed significantly improved abilities in math and improvement in thinking skills in general during her sixth-grade year. Having received straight A's on her report card, she received a letter of invitation to join the National Junior Honor Society at her school. At home, she frequently figured out how to play songs on her violin by ear, instead of only playing from a sheet of music. Although her weakest subject was math, her sixth-grade math teacher commented that Nicole was "one of the stronger math students in the class." At the end of the school year, she tested as above grade level in math, reading and writing. Math and reading scores at the end of sixth grade are shown in the following graphs (the thick, bold line is Nicole's; the other two lines on each graph represent district and normal averages for the same grade levels). In a three-year period Nicole advanced from below grade level to considerably above grade level in math. Her improvement in math during the second semester of sixth grade was substantial enough to be noticed and acknowledged by the principal, who had 700 students in her school! Nicole's reading scores were consistently above grade level and, it is interesting to note, the scores show that her rate of progression exceeded that of her peers.

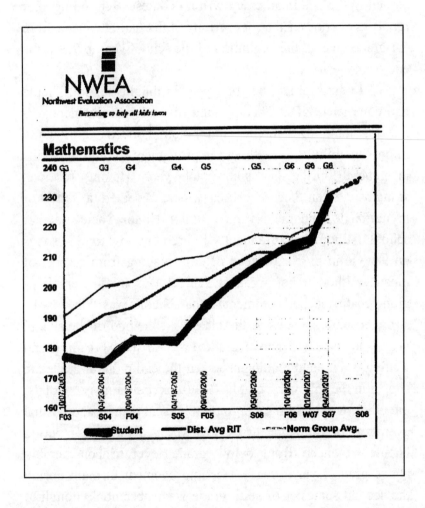

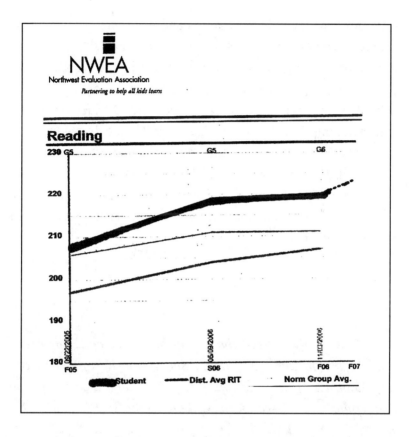

She continues to excel in violin lessons at school, and she was placed in an advanced language arts class as a seventh grader. She has been a member of a summer swim team for two years, enjoys riding her bicycle, has competed in three kids' triathlons and regularly wins medals for placing in the top three in her age group at local 5K and 10K running races. Nicole enjoys babysitting and pet sitting for neighbors, and she is an active Girl Scout. She is a true "people person" who is quick to give hugs and makes friends very easily. She is outgoing and sociable with adults and her peers—a very well-rounded young lady. In a recent poem that she wrote for homework, Nicole described herself as "joyful." She is both joyful and a joy to know. Two-and-a-half months into the school year, her seventh-grade science teacher sent the following unsolicited e-mail message to Nicole's mother:

> I just wanted to say how much of a pleasure it has been to teach [Nicole] this year. She is creative, ambitious, curious and very knowledgeable about the material. I am looking forward to what [Nicole] can produce.

"I firmly believe that Anna has drastically improved [Nicole]'s life and her future. She is more capable, more confident, less frustrated and incredibly more successful than she could ever have been without Anna's therapies. Our family is so grateful that we found Anna. I wish that every child could have the chance to benefit from her work."

Nicole's mother

Seth

Prior interventions with Sensory Integration, occupational therapy, speech therapy, Samonas Sound Therapy and neurological chiropractic care

This is a truly fascinating story about an exceptionally bright seven-and-a-half-year-old boy who was unable to manifest his true potential. Knowing him as I do now, I wonder what would have become of him had his mother not continually pursued answers to his difficulties. This boy is truly gifted intellectually, yet the dysfunction in his central nervous system drastically interfered with his ability to function. During our initial meeting, he sat on the floor and continually spun in circles. Momentarily he stopped, and I attempted to engage him in conversation. His eyes rolled in circles, and he made animal-like noises. I could not engage him in any sort of dialogue. It intrigued me and I suspected that this was not a boy who struggled with self-control; this was a boy who was extremely uncomfortable in the given situation.

His mother said he not only displayed quite immature behavior, but he also showed no interest in learning to read or write. Yet he knew all about dinosaurs and could answer trivia-type questions about any kind of dinosaur. How could he know so much about dinosaurs and yet show such limited abilities in remembering his ABC's? His mother shared the following:

As an infant, [Seth] could only nurse in a completely silent and dimly lit room. When he started on solid food, he would turn his head to the wall and cry when the meal was presented to him. I told my concerns to our pediatrician on several occasions, but since [Seth]'s development (according to the charts) was on target, everything appeared to be normal. It was also difficult for me to know what to expect because [Seth] was my first child. Later I began to notice other behaviors that were upsetting, such as crying and screaming when combing his hair, or brushing his teeth, and even when changing his clothes. He was sensitive to light, and would become stiff and hostile if people came close to him.

I was given plenty of advice on picky eaters, and even more advice on how to be a "better parent." By 18 months of age, and with these behaviors progressing, [Seth]'s weight plummeted dangerously low, and he was finally sent to a pediatric feeding specialist ... From this, I learned that his eating issues were due to a larger problem they labeled Sensory Integration Disorder, more commonly known as SI. I researched SI and was overwhelmed with the implications for my son's future. I asked myself questions like: "How do I parent when I'm unsure if he's acting out (having a tantrum) for a legitimate reason, or if it's normal childlike behavior that calls for discipline?" And "Is he screaming because he simply doesn't want to put on a jacket, or does it really hurt him?" I also wondered, "How do I explain his behavior to someone who is unfamiliar with the disorder?" ...

Along with tactile defensiveness, [Seth] had poor spatial awareness and difficulty following instructions; he needed constant movement, had mood swings and displayed emotional instability. I began taking him to an occupational therapist (OT) trained in Sensory Integration ... He became less sensitive to touch, but still suffered emotional meltdowns in which he would start crying and throwing fits over what seemed to be trivial reasons. Some of his frustration was due to his unintelligible speech. By this time, [Seth] was almost three and extremely intelligent, but unable to articulate his ideas clearly.

In conjunction with occupational therapy, I started [Seth] in speech therapy at Children's Hospital. The speech therapists worked at strengthening the muscles in [Seth]'s mouth; I was told that the main problem was not his inability to talk clearly, but the inability of his brain to pull everything together so words could come out appropriately. While undergoing speech therapy, [Seth] actually had to discontinue the OT because his sensory problems became more extreme. The OT explained that [Seth] could only handle work on one area at a time, so I concentrated on the speech therapy. When his speech improved, I started up the OT again. We utilized Child Find, a government program for children needing special services, and then private therapy with a new OT because we had switched insurance companies. However, after a year of private OT, I learned that the therapist's aim was to give [Seth] future coping skills, not to effect permanent change.

So I returned to the earlier therapist, trained in SI, who had a more progressive perspective. [Seth] was re-evaluated, and she came up with a strategy, which included individual therapy, group therapy and cranial sacral adjustments. For the group therapy I was able to enroll my son in a public preschool group for children with early learning delays. The teachers were trained therapists in speech and motor skills. The school evaluation showed [Seth] to be delayed, but exceptionally bright. He could remember numerous facts on whatever happened to be his latest fascination. He also built a swinging pendulum out of magnets, and loved to sit and be read to for hours. But, when it came to writing, he was definitely behind. He cried if anyone tried to make him color, much less write. Yet, it seemed that with the help of the school and the Sensory Integration therapy, he was making certain gains. His tactile defensiveness, which made him not want to hold a pencil (because of the feeling it created), had subsided. He started enjoying coloring for the first time, but by the end of the school year, at the age of five, he was still unable to write his name. His school therapist was puzzled as to where the breakdown was occurring, since he clearly knew his letters and had the physical ability to write. She thought he might possibly need vision therapy, but his vision was found to be normal.

Through his SI therapist, [Seth] started Samonas Sound Therapy. Samonas uses specially designed music, sounds and tones to stimulate responses in the brain. [Seth] was able to do this at home with specialized headphones on a portable CD player. Although [Seth] hated doing the sound therapy, it seemed to have strong effects on his behavior. We experienced good weeks where he was very calm, but this deteriorated into constant emotional meltdowns. His therapist did make changes in his program, but it was based more upon her intuition than on concrete knowledge of the therapy's effects on the brain. His behavior became even more erratic, and I decided to stop the sound therapy.

From an outside perspective, [Seth] may have seemed undisciplined, but I knew he was actually trying to compensate for a lack of control over his own body. When he had emotional meltdowns, he would sob and tell me that he "was trying really hard not to cry." It was heartbreaking to see him struggling so hard. I started home-schooling him because I knew he would have difficulties in a regular school setting. Academic issues became increasingly obvious: letters he had previously learned were forgotten or reversed, he begged me to let him stop writing after just a few letters and schooling became a constant battle. My husband, who had always had a hard time admitting that [Seth] had real problems, made the battle even more difficult. He struggled with believing that [Seth]'s academic and behavioral difficulties were related to physical or neurological problems. (Even though he was not supportive of [Seth]'s therapies, he tolerated them as long as he did not have to participate.) Seeking help, I set an appointment with a chiropractor certified in chiropractic neurology. Through his evaluation, the chiropractor determined that [Seth]'s brain had been over-stimulated and that there was an imbalance between the left and right hemispheres, which affected his learning. I started taking [Seth] to the chiropractor regularly, but by this time I was pregnant with our fourth child, and, without help, it was hard for me to stay consistent with his appointments...

By th[e] time [Seth] was six, [he] had been through so many therapies, [yet] I knew there was still an underlying piece of the problem that had not been addressed. I also knew that [Seth] was not simply misbehaving, and I wanted him to have more than coping skills. Moreover, the older he grew, the more apparent it became that his struggles with reading and writing would affect his future success. So with all of this in mind, I had [Seth] evaluated by Anna.

My initial assessment with Seth showed that all of the primitive reflexes were fully retained or nearly fully retained and the postural reflexes were completely underdeveloped. His face, arms and legs recognized human touch only when firm pressure was applied. He showed extreme difficulty maintaining balance in a standing-still position, which became impossible when he closed his eyes. His eye movements were extremely impaired as he could not fixate on an object, his eyes did not converge and he could not track or hand-eye track. His pencil grip was extremely weak, and he struggled to shape his letters, as in the following example:

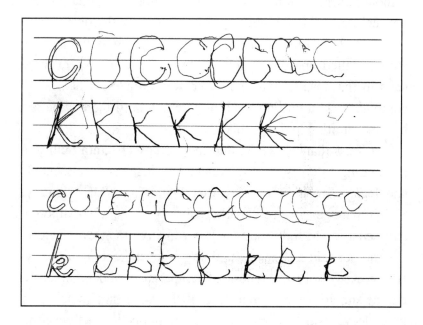

I suggested that his mother delay having him do any reading or writing until things improved.

During the following year, as Seth systematically progressed through NDD Therapy, I gradually observed changes and noted his mother's observations as well. After his first few days of NDD Therapy, his mother noticed a temporary increase in sensitivity to textures, tastes and emotions. Within eight weeks of starting NDD Therapy, Seth was able to sit still in a chair and converse with me. His mother began observing more stable and calmer behavior. His high emotional states began to diminish in frequency. His response to pain, however, was still abnormal in that he did not feel pain or touch until it was severe or with considerable pressure. Two months after I began working with him his mother called one day to tell me that he had just spent three days in the hospital with an abscessed tooth. Seth had never complained of a hurting tooth or sore jaw until the day before he was admitted to the hospital.

Less than 12 weeks into the therapy program Seth was responding to the softest of touches on his face, arms, hands and legs. And four months after beginning NDD Therapy, Seth no longer showed over-sensitivity to sound. Although still sensitive to light, he was less sensitive than ever before. His mother said he was maintaining an even keel emotionally. He showed more awareness of temperature and commented that he should wear pants instead of shorts, or that he needed a long-sleeved shirt. Mom also said she noticed a difference in Seth's eyes: "He's more focused, and his eye contact is significantly improved."

Five months after beginning NDD Therapy, I met a friend of Seth's family, and she shared with me observations of her own. She said he was calmer, more aware of his surroundings and much more engaging. She noticed an increased level of maturity. Seth tested as having significant inhibition of several primitive reflexes, especially the Moro, TLR, Rooting, Sucking, Palmar and Spinal Galant. His balance had improved so that he was now able to stand still with his feet together, as well as stand on one foot for 30 seconds, normal for his age. His eye movements had improved phenomenally. I no longer saw difficulty with fixation or convergence. His eye tracking and hand-eye tracking had progressed nicely, but still needed improvement. Based on eye movement stability, Seth was ready to start reading; his listening skills were still poor, however, so I did not want him to start reading just yet. Discrimination between sounds was quite difficult for him, which would complicate reading. Appropriately, Seth was ready to start a Listening Fitness Program.

Mom noticed new and significant changes in her son almost immediately upon starting the listening therapy. His appetite became enormous; she had never seen anything like it. Dad agreed. She said previously she had to force him to eat, and suddenly he was eating three bowls of cereal and/or oatmeal every morning. Mom said Seth seemed happier and more at peace within himself than she had ever seen. "Now when he is emotional it isn't with anger—he's still 'sweet.'" About half way through the listening therapy, Seth's appetite subdued some and he temporarily struggled with getting to sleep at night. He was able to sleep late into the morning, though, which was new for him. At this same time he began riding a two-wheeled bicycle for the first time.

After completing 60 hours of the Listening Fitness Program and continuing with NDD Therapy, Seth became quite adept at riding his bicycle, and he began taking an interest in drawing and tracing pictures. Mom started working with him on sounds of the alphabet. She soon noticed discrimination difficulties with certain sounds, so Seth completed a 20-hour listening Boost. Later, testing showed he was now able to distinguish between specific sounds of letters, speak with good articulation, follow directions without having them repeated several times, follow multiple instructions, demonstrate a longer attention span and begin to read and write. Even though his drawings still showed delay, his ability to control a pencil was improving.

Three months later, as Seth continued NDD Therapy, his mother began implementing my reading/spelling/writing curriculum. Seth was a beginner reader, starting to read consonant-vowel-consonant words. His mother shared the following:

> When [Seth] came to the point in therapy where I could begin schooling again, he was still sobbing when doing his work. I brought my concerns to Anna, who without hesitation confirmed he was within his capabilities to start reading and writing. In [Seth]'s previous therapies I frequently asked the therapists how I would know the difference between legitimate behaviors or defiance with [Seth]. The answer had basically been there was no way to tell. Now, armed with Anna's reassurance that [Seth] was simply misbehaving, I asked him if he could not do the work or just did not want to. To my surprise, he openly told me that he just did not want to do it. That moment was such a breakthrough for me because it gave me the confidence to parent without fear of damaging my son with unrealistic expectations.

Significant improvement had taken place with Seth's ATNR. His eye tracking and hand-eye tracking were much smoother. He demonstrated good pencil control and he began to draw and shape letters. One day he brought me the following picture, which he copied from a book without tracing. His sudden ability to draw with detail and proportion was astounding. Seth drew the following picture only three months after the drawing on page 84!

One month later, shortly after turning eight, Seth brought me the following paper he wrote only four months after learning to correctly hold a pencil and shape letters. The rhymes are his own.

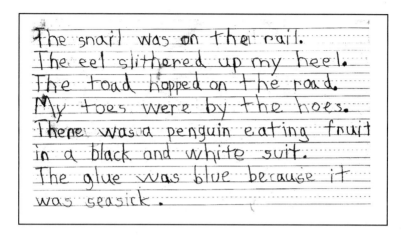

The snail was on the rail.
The eel slithered up my heel.
The toad hopped on the road.
My toes were by the hoes.
There was a penguin eating fruit
in a black and white suit.
The glue was blue because it
was seasick.

Seth's academics were progressing at a phenomenal rate. His mother shared the following:

> As we progressed with Anna's therapy, she closely monitored [Seth]'s progress. I had noticed at home that he was unable to read larger words, even though he knew all the sounds in a word. I did not think to mention this to Anna, but noticed on the way home, after a session with her, that he was reading signs everywhere such as "Learning Express" and "Happy Holidays." The next day I told Anna that I had no idea what she had done in the last session, but he was reading large words! Anna expressed that she had seen the light bulb come on in her last session with [Seth], and that she was glad to hear it had been confirmed.

Within just eight months of beginning to read short simple words, Seth was reading junior adult fiction books. I was thrilled one day when he brought me a copy of *Eragon*, by Christopher Paolini, and read a few pages to me. The academic progress this boy made in less than a year was phenomenal. His mother said she was amazed at his reading and comprehension levels.

I tremendously enjoy visiting with Seth when he comes to see me. He'll walk in with a book, sit in a chair, cross one leg over the other and begin telling me about what he's been reading. He said to his mother one day, "Why would I watch TV when I can read a book?"

Seth is a delightful, brilliant, now-nine-year-old boy. He no longer demonstrates tactile sensitivity, sensory integration difficulties or other aberrant behaviors. He is above grade level academically and loves learning. Eighteen months after beginning to read and write for the first time, he was formally tested, by an independent tester, using the Woodcock Johnson Test. He tested at sixth-grade level in reading and 3.1 grade level in writing. He advanced six grade levels in reading and three grade levels in writing in only 18 months! His mother had given him a home-school break from writing for a few months prior to the testing. Having seen his astounding test results, she was more excited than ever to encourage Seth to bring his writing skills closer to that of his reading skills. Now he is learning to write paragraphs. Following are four samples of Seth's writing, less than two years after learning to hold a pencil and shape the letters of the alphabet.

We got our dog Moby one Sunday in April. His owners were getting rid of him because they were not home enough to spend time with him. We think Moby is a mix of a chocolate lab and a pointer. He is a medium sized dog. I enjoy playing fetch with Moby and taking him for walks. Moby's eyes always look sad when we are eating dinner he begs for food. When Moby sees squirrels and rabbits he barks at them. Moby is our first dog and I can't imagine life without him.

Near my house I ride my bike on sand dunes. I call them sand dunes because they are big hills made out of sand and packed dirt. The sand is a reddish brown, and when I ride on them I get really dirty. Many bike tires have made thin trails on the hills. The trails let your bike go really fast. There are also many ramps for jumping. Some times the jump is smooth like ripples and other times like rough waves. Bike riding on the sand dunes is fun.

Spring is a great season. The weather is perfect for bike riding because it is not too hot and not too cold. There is a trail with noisy prairie dogs on each side that we like to ride on. When it rains we have fun playing outside. My brother, sisters, and I put buckets underneath the gutters to catch the rain, and play with the water. Easter is my favorite part of spring because this is when we celebrate Jesus giving up his life for us. We make special eggs called cascarones wich are hollowed, dyed, and filled with glitter. On Easter we throw the cascarones at a wall and shout, "Christ has risen." Spring is the perfect time for outside activities and Easter.

Our museum has a fantastic display of gems and minerals. There is a window where you can see the inside of a cave made of sparkling white crystals. The crystals grow on the walls, floor, and ceiling of the cave. Another area is full of different shaped pieces of gold. They have gold as thin as paper, gold that looks like silver, and gold nuggets. They also have a display of cut gems. There are gems of almost every color and some are very valuable. My favorite exhibit in the museum is the gems and minerals.

Seth is nearing completion of NDD Therapy; he is currently working to develop the postural reflexes, which seem to be contributing to development of his reasoning skills. His mother recently purchased a dictionary for Seth. He was so thrilled with it that he carried it with him when they traveled in the car. He enjoys learning about words and their origins. The problem his mother now has is staying one step ahead of him:

Today, [Seth] is no longer defensive to touch, he smiles all the time and rarely has emotional meltdowns. I can take him places without fear of him losing control, and I enjoy seeing him confidently interact with people. My husband and I are proud of [Seth]'s academic gains. What Anna gives me today is invaluable, a solid measurement of how far [Seth] has come, and hope for how far he will go.

Recently Seth's mother also shared the following:

My son came to me one evening around 8:30. He told me he had finished all his library books, was a little bored and wanted to know if he could "write the body of a paragraph." It is hard to believe that this is from a child who months earlier would whine and fight at the mention of writing. Not only has he taken off in his writing, but he absolutely loves it. Instead of complaining how long a paragraph is to write, he proudly shows me how much of the paper he has filled. Instead of a battle to get him going, he is so excited that he plans out what he wants to write the next day.

Through our work with Anna, [Seth] has taken off in ways I never thought possible; but more importantly, I see the self-esteem he has gained, the eagerness he has to learn, and now the ability to do just that.

"[Anna] validated [Seth]'s struggles and his behaviors by telling me the physical reasons behind them. Her extensive experience and compassion as a mother gave me the hope that [Seth] could reach his potential. I was crying by the time I left our first meeting. Her approach to my son was completely different from anything I had experienced."

Seth's mother

Miranda

Previous diagnoses of slight Dyslexia and auditory processing difficulties, with prior interventions including brain integration therapy

A sweet, quiet girl, Miranda first came to see me shortly after turning nine, towards the end of third grade. Mom said that Miranda's preschool and kindergarten teachers had noticed problems with Miranda's motor skill development. She had suffered numerous ear infections between the ages of four and six, but otherwise she seemed to be a normal, healthy, happy child. Miranda's mother says this:

> We noticed in second grade that [Miranda] had troubles with reading and writing skills, so we started investigating what we could do to help her. We also observed an inability to explain situations, describe events very well or express herself in complete sentences. If we asked her what she had for lunch that day, we would wait 45 seconds to one minute in silence before she would say anything, and then it wouldn't be very descriptive.

We had her eyesight checked and learned that she was not using both eyes to focus; rather, she was switching back and forth between them constantly, which made tracking while reading almost impossible. She was prescribed glasses and we began some eye tracking exercises. We also started some brain integration therapy, which consisted of about six different daily exercises. It made a huge impact, but I discovered that when we stopped the exercises the problems would return. For example, b's and d's were often reversed.

Following is a sample of Miranda's writing near the end of second grade. Her writing did not improve in third grade.

As a third-grade student, Miranda was a cheerful, calm child. She was active in ballet lessons, involved in church activities and loved art and music. Her difficulties appeared to be primarily related to academics, although she did show slightly slower gross motor coordination for her age. She reversed letters and words, was a whole word reader and was in special education for reading and writing. Academically, she tested as one full year behind.

I started an NDD Therapy program with Miranda when she was in her last month of third grade. She tested as having the following aberrant reflexes: Moro, Rooting, Sucking, Palmar, Plantar, TLR, ATNR and STNR as well as underdeveloped postural reflexes. Her eye tracking was slightly impaired, and hand-eye tracking and convergence were both impaired. During our first few visits, Miranda sat with her head held downward. She showed little or no eye contact, although she politely conversed with me and answered my questions. I asked her to write a sentence of her own—whatever she wanted to write. This is what she wrote:

I asked Miranda to read her sentence to me and she said, "I am bored." Quite often, I have noticed that children with writing difficulties omit articles, verbs, correct verb tenses, and/or appropriate suffixes.

Two months after starting NDD Therapy, Miranda was developmentally ready to start a 60-hour Listening Fitness Program. Her auditory testing had shown that she experienced difficulties with discriminating between sounds in words, she was easily distracted by sound and she struggled with auditory memory.

During the listening therapy and while continuing NDD Therapy, Miranda began to blossom. Her mother shared that Miranda was noticeably more expressive, "She talks all the time, and even sings with the radio in the car." She became talkative at the dinner table with the family, and people made comments to Mom that Miranda seemed more outgoing. Towards the end of the Listening Fitness Program, Miranda shared with me that she could understand and comprehend better when people spoke to her. Mom agreed and said she seemed to be processing better. I noticed her head had come up and direct eye contact was made when she greeted me.

The following fall, after a month-and-a-half of fourth grade, Miranda's reading showed significant improvement. Her writing drastically improved. Miranda shared that sometimes she wants to write and write and write, which was new for her. Following is a sample:

> *Writing*
>
> !! Jolly Rancher!!
>
> What is that cool candy?
> Wow! It tastes like a cherry!
> This little candy is called a
> Jolly Rancher. It's smooth, red
> and edible. The wrapper is wrinkly,
> the candy is sticky and hard.
> The red Jolly Rancher smells sweet
> like cherries. When I drop it
> on my besk it sound's like
> "tink, tink, tink." When I taste
> it, it tastes like cherries and
> watery.

When I re-tested Miranda, I found that her balance had significantly improved. The Moro, Rooting, Sucking, Palmar and Plantar reflexes showed inhibition. Her hand-eye tracking had significantly improved, and she showed no difficulties with convergence.

During her winter break from school, Miranda completed 20 hours of a listening Boost to further enhance auditory discrimination. A few months afterward, her mother said she was doing really well in school and "from what I can tell on her homework and CSAP testing, I think we might be able to catch her up this year! I am so excited for her!" Miranda's reading had become more fluid; she was reading more difficult material, and she was reading independently.

One year after Miranda began NDD Therapy, she tested as having inhibited all of the primitive reflexes. Her eye convergence, eye tracking and hand-eye tracking were smooth and fluid. She tested as having none of the auditory difficulties she originally demonstrated.

Her mother shared that Miranda had been accepted into Dennison School for the following school year. Dennison School is an option school that demands high standards and provides a traditional approach to education. Miranda was academically tested by Dennison school and found to be just a few months behind for an ending fourth grader—she had advanced two grade levels in one year! Her mother said, "...this has been an incredible journey to watch … The more that can be done early on for a child, the better off the child will be later … the increase in self-esteem and confidence is wonderful to experience."

Following is an example of Miranda's writing as a fifth-grade student:

The Digestive System

The first time I had a terrible nightmare in a deep away sleep I was a berry and found myself in the digestive system. It all started in the mouth with the teeth chomping down on me like a saw shattering wood into little pieces. Then, there was the tongue. The tongue was like a machine itching my back. After the mouth, which was the worst, I went through the esophagus.

Wo, Wo - the esophagus was pulling me down like the world's fastest rollercoaster. After my favorite part, I went in the stomach. The way back to the esophagus was closed now, and it was pitch dark. I started to spin in circles and suddenly

turned into a nasty paste.
After the squashing stomach, I
went into the small intestine
with the swirling villis. The
villis, certainly gave me a
headache. Then part of me
was gone, I went on the way
out of the villis I went into
the big intestine; it was enormous
and wide,

Now, there was nothing left of me, I fell
in a puddle and never saw
daylight again.

Do you know what the puddle of
water was? When I woke up
I found myself in the
bathroom. Oooopppsssss!

When Miranda finished her fifth-grade year, her mother shared with me that it was an extremely exciting time for both mother and daughter. Miranda's fifth-grade Colorado Student Assessment Program (CSAP) testing showed that she performed at proficient levels in all areas tested. Miranda's summer between fifth and sixth grades was the first summer she spent time strengthening her academic skills instead of focusing on remedial reading and writing.

Miranda's mother was so fascinated by her daughter's developmental progress and academic achievement that she has decided to change her career within the next several years. She has enrolled as a student at a nearby university and is seeking a degree in education with the hopes of later acquiring certification as an NDD therapist and as a Listening Fitness instructor. In a recent paper for one of her classes, she wrote the following:

> [T]he opportunity to take my own daughter through such "A non-invasive approach to solving learning and behavior problems" (by Sally Goddard, *Reflexes, Learning and Behavior,* 2nd edition, 2005, Eugene, Fern Ridge Press), as well as through some other tactical programs such as the Listening Fitness Program, demonstrated to me that these programs applied in the *proper order* will work wonderfully in helping children reach their educational goals of performing at grade level in a relatively short period of time. [Miranda]'s third grade standard assessment tests showed her reading level at first grade, whereas her

fifth grade CSAP tests showed her proficient in all areas at the fifth grade level.

In a recent conversation with Miranda's mother, she shared her latest observation. She said Miranda always used to struggle with understanding cause-and-effect and deductive reasoning. In a recent family discussion, however, Miranda entered the conversation with a comment suggesting, "If such and such happens…, then that would mean …." Her mother was quite surprised that Miranda processed the logical consequences of the situation and verbalized it very succinctly. Developmental growth continues.

"The two programs that Anna combined to overcome developmental issues have played an important part in getting [Miranda] onto the right path for success. Together with focused academic instruction, it has been an incredible journey to watch. I would recommend any parents have their child evaluated. The more that can be done early on the better off the child will be later, down the road. It takes dedication from all parties, but it is worthwhile because the increase in a child's self-esteem and confidence is wonderful to experience."

Miranda's mother

Heather

Previous diagnosis of Perceptual Communication Disorder, with prior interventions including private tutoring, vision therapy and the Davis Dyslexia Correction Program

This beautiful girl had been a reading student of mine when she was nine years old. She had dyslexic tendencies and was simultaneously involved in vision therapy. I remember it was quite difficult for her to grasp and retain phonetic sounds. We drilled, used picture words and emphasized sounds— everything I could creatively come up with to help her read. Nothing lasted. What she learned one day was quickly forgotten. She improved some, but not to my satisfaction.

Once I became certified as an NDD therapist, I had immediate recollections of Heather and called her mother. One of the things I most remembered about Heather was that she regularly fell off chairs. We would be working at a desk or sitting on chairs across from each other, and without any inducement at all, she was suddenly on the floor. As a newly-trained NDD therapist, I wondered if Heather might have Neuro-Developmental Delay.

Heather was born at 35 weeks with the cord wrapped twice around her neck. She was colicky and had many ear infections in her early life. By the time she was 11 years old, she had already been through tutoring, vision therapy and the Davis Dyslexia Correction Program. Her school had diagnosed her as having Perceptual Communication Disorder, and as a fifth grader, she was on an Individualized Educational Plan (IEP). Her reading was extremely poor, and her writing was illegible.

Heather's parents had her evaluated by The Denver Gifted Development Center and the Colorado State University Fort Collins Center for Auditory Processing Research. The Gifted Development Center suggested that Heather is a visual-spatial learner, and the Central Auditory Processing evaluation reported that her auditory system functions were within normal ranges in all areas tested.

Heather's parents were deeply concerned about her future regarding her reading and writing. She was a happy, well-adjusted girl, very athletic and coordinated. Yet her academic levels were extremely low.

I tested Heather and began an NDD Therapy program with her when she was just shy of turning 12. Her assessment showed strong TLR, ATNR and STNR primitive reflexes, and underdeveloped postural reflexes. Her eye tracking was good as long as she could devote all of her concentration to it without any cognitive involvement; hand-eye tracking was a struggle, and vertical tracking was difficult. She showed mixed laterality rather than one-side dominance (no dominant hand, foot, eye or ear). Most significant was that she showed mixed-ear dominance. Noise was distracting to her, and my testing showed auditory processing difficulties.

Within the first six to 12 weeks of NDD Therapy, her mother noticed improved balance and muscle tone. She told me that Heather, who could ride a bicycle at the age of five, was now riding her bicycle without hands for the first time. Heather began demonstrating improved muscle tone in her sitting posture. Her back was straighter, and she had better form overall.

Six months later, Heather's NDD re-testing showed significant inhibition of the TLR, ATNR and STNR. The head righting postural reflexes were nearly fully developed. Eye tracking and hand-eye tracking were smooth. Heather then began a 60-hour Listening Fitness Program and brought me a current sample of her writing (age 12).

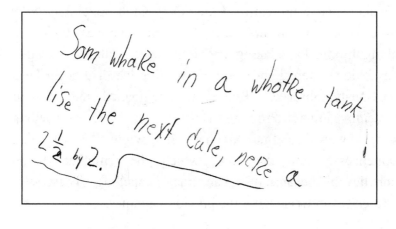

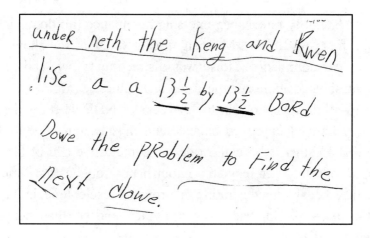

In addition to mixed-ear dominance, she struggled with discrimination of specific sounds in words, which directly affected her spelling. She also consistently chose visual cues over auditory cues. As we worked on discrimination of letter sounds, Heather said to me one day, "I didn't know the letters of the alphabet make such similar sounds."

Reading and writing began to change dramatically. Heather picked up and read the young adult novel *Nightjohn* by Gary Paulsen in three days. Mom said she was staying up at night to read and taking a book in the car with her to read—an obvious interest and ability in reading that had never been previously observed. Before we completed the 60-hour Listening Fitness Program, Heather was correctly spelling simple words, a first for her. She wrote the following sentences from dictation, which her mother found unbelievable because of the accuracy in spelling. These were written seven weeks after the previous samples.

1. A rabbit was by the cactus.

2. The children will cut the pumpkin up for Mom.

3. Jill put a sandwich and muffin in the lunch basket.

4. The chipmunk sat on a log to munch on his nuts.

5. I can add and subtract in math.

6. Jan put a velvet ribbon on the red bonnet.

7. Brant did a hundred math problems.

8. We had a fun picnic until ants and insects got into the lunch basket.

Heather shared with me that this was the best her spelling had ever been, and, for the first time in her life, she was excited about being asked to spell words. Mom began implementing my reading/spelling/writing curriculum as part of Heather's home-schooling.

Three months after completing the Listening Fitness Program, and while continuing with NDD Therapy, Heather's mother called me one day. She excitedly shared that the previous night the family had gone to a restaurant for dinner and Heather read descriptions of various menu items by herself for the first time. Mom had expected she would read the menu to Heather, as she had always done when they occasionally ate out.

One year after beginning NDD Therapy, Heather tested as having completely inhibited all of the primitive reflexes. All but one of the postural reflexes had developed, and she decided to work through the final one on her own. Her eye movements are stable and smooth. Heather continues to improve in reading and writing. She enjoys independent reading for pleasure. Her mother says she has significantly improved in her ability to take legible notes while listening to teachers. Heather now considers herself a reader—not someone who is limited to sounding out and deciphering words, but someone who can read for meaning and enjoyment. Her spelling is continuing to improve, with no dyslexic tendencies whatsoever. She recently obtained a manual for a motorized water safety course, studied it for one week and then took a four-page written test—and passed. At age 14 she was licensed to drive jet skis and boats.

Caleb

Previous diagnoses of subtle central auditory processing difficulties and Twice-Exceptional, visual-spatial learner, with prior interventions including private tutoring and vision therapy

Heather's younger brother Caleb struggled with body awareness, coordination, balance, muscle tone, eye movements, delayed processing and spatial awareness. During her pregnancy, Caleb's mother experienced a threatened miscarriage and pre-term labor. Caleb was born with the cord wrapped around his neck. Although he began to walk and talk a bit early, his sensory-motor development was delayed and he had poor core strength. He disliked having his hair brushed and demonstrated scalp sensitivity. During his early school years he was diagnosed with mild auditory processing disorder and experienced 18 months of vision therapy.

Caleb struggled academically. His first- through third-grade teachers all said he had difficulty sitting still and he struggled with staying on task. Caleb became a target for bullies and began a special education Individualized Educational Plan (IEP). Although his school work started out at grade level, he needed more time in order to complete his assignments. He did not like playing ball activities, continued to struggle with sitting still and was not motivated to do homework. His best subjects were math and science, and his worst was writing.

Caleb was noticeably loyal, kind, curious, happy and creative, but he was immature for his age. He often overreacted to sudden, unexpected noise and did not adjust to body space. He would often invade the body space of others. He had no sense of balance or anticipation of movement. His mother said he was not able to read body language, had difficulty making friends, had a poor self-image and tended to withdraw and avoid others. His mother said, "If there is a change in routine for more than two days, like a really busy weekend that includes a change in diet, it's common for Caleb to get a headache and occasionally vomit."

Caleb's school informed his parents that he easily became overwhelmed with reading and writing tasks. By third grade he tested below grade level in reading and writing and needed extended time to complete tests. Timing frustrated him, and he seemed to process slower than others. Spelling was a challenge, and it took him a long time to copy from an overhead. He struggled with putting ideas into writing. If over-stimulated or overwhelmed, he tended to fail. He was provided a central auditory filter to wear on his ear but did not want to wear it.

Colorado State University Fort Collins Center for Auditory Processing Research performed a central auditory processing evaluation and determined that Caleb not only needed to wear a filter on his ear, but also required taking tests in a separate, quiet room. In addition, earmuffs were to be worn during desk activities and when testing. The Denver Gifted Development Center diagnosed him as Twice-Exceptional (gifted with disabilities) and suggested that Caleb be taught to his visual-spatial strengths. His mother remarked to me, "How can he be gifted when he doesn't seem to have any common sense?"

I evaluated Caleb when he was almost 10 years old and in fourth grade. He was a happy, friendly boy. Initial observation showed he was completely lacking in muscle tone. He could not sit on the floor without back support. When I asked him to sit up and then removed my hand from his back, he fell over onto his side. His NDD assessment showed retained Moro, Rooting, TLR, Spinal Galant and ATNR primitive reflexes, and the postural reflexes were absent. His hand-eye tracking was extremely poor. Visual-perceptual skills were poor, and he showed significant auditory processing difficulties.

A few days after beginning NDD Therapy, Caleb's mother noticed that he seemed more fatigued than usual. He tired very quickly on a short walk. Yet one month later his mother noticed Caleb no longer seemed as fatigued when taking walks. When standing, he began to hold his head straight, rather than tilted to one side. He became a little more aware of his own space when walking next to Mom. He began sleeping later into the morning, while before he had always been up and active by 6:30 a.m. His mother also observed:

[Caleb] has always had a very sensitive scalp. When he concentrates on school work, I notice him pulling on his bangs. Also, brushing his hair has always been somewhat of a fight. He complains that it hurts. I have noticed that brushing is more tolerable lately.

A month later his mother sent me an e-mail:

> On our vacation we swam every night. [Caleb] spent most of the time playing catch with a football. I originally thought it was because he didn't have anything else to do and that his dad would play with him. But, this week he has been playing catch with the other kids on the block. Last night I had to make him stop when it was dark. This is a huge thing for him!! He would always go along with a friend for five minutes or so but was never really interested in throwing or catching for too long. Also he is really catching the ball. With vision therapy we saw some change—at least he could occasionally catch the ball, but not very often. This is different. He is getting in the middle of the group and going for the ball!! WOW! Maybe I'm making more of this than there is, but he has never done this before. He was somewhat competitive!! I guess what I saw more than anything is that he was in control of his body.

Four-and-a-half months after beginning NDD Therapy, testing showed that Caleb had made remarkable progress with inhibition of the TLR, Plantar, Rooting and Spinal Galant reflexes. Caleb's mother noticed he had begun demonstrating good posture when writing and engaging in schoolwork: "He sits up now and uses a good pencil grip. No more lying his head down on the table." A few days later she added:

> The family just realized yesterday that [Caleb] has not had a migraine headache in the last three months or so. He usually has them quite often, and they are completely debilitating and sometimes cause vomiting. Significantly improved posture, too!

Two weeks later, Mom said:

> I have noticed that [Caleb] doesn't make noise constantly. I can't say when this happened—just that I don't notice it any more. He did have two days in which he had a headache, though on day one I was busy and didn't realize until it was too late that he had been watching TV a lot. I have to note that his headache was less intense, no nausea or vomiting, and he didn't need to go to bed to get relief. My big clue something was going on was that he was having a difficult time staying on task and following directions. When I asked him what was up he said, "My head just hurts." Wow! In the past he would be crying and rubbing his head on the furniture and hands (kind of like burrowing).

Six months after starting NDD Therapy, Caleb's tests showed complete inhibition of the Moro, Palmar, Plantar, Rooting, and Spinal Galant reflexes. His head righting postural reflexes had completely developed. We then began a 60-hour Listening Fitness Program.

After his first week of the listening therapy, Mom asked Caleb if he had noticed anything yet. He said he could hear better than before (his third day on the program he told me he noticed he could hear better). Mom added that before beginning the listening therapy, Caleb would pull his head away fearfully any time she put her hand near his ears. Now she can tickle him right next to his ear and on the tip of his earlobe, and he laughs.

During Caleb's second week of the listening therapy Mom said:

> [Caleb] is more focused, more aware of what is going on around him. As he was going upstairs this morning his sister asked him to bring down a pair of socks for her when he came back down. Usually this would overwhelm him and he would be unable to do what he needed to do and then bring something for his sister. This morning it was no problem at all.

One evening Caleb's mother called to share that earlier when she had called Caleb downstairs, he opened his bedroom door and answered her right away. She said she'd *never* seen him do this—it had always taken at least four or five calls before he responded. After dinner she called him while he was listening to a book on tape and again he answered right away.

Halfway through the Listening Fitness Program, his mother said:

[Caleb]'s "Darth Vader" voice is gone. He no longer talks with a congested, heavy-breathing nasally sound. He is also reading in a much more fluid manner.

Within a few days I received an e-mail from his mother:

One of [Caleb]'s little quirks is gone. It was much more than a quirk. [Caleb] is no longer walking into the personal space of other people!!!! I have suspected this for about a month but have not had an opportunity to really watch him. We went shopping last week and, lo and behold, [Caleb] was not on top of me or in the path of the cart!!! I also had a friend visit me last week, and she made a comment that [Caleb] just seems more mature and that he has blossomed.

After a year of NDD Therapy and having completed the Listening Fitness Program, Caleb's mother commented:

It used to be when I combed [Caleb]'s hair before school he winced and pulled away with every stroke of the brush, along with vocal complaints. He just doesn't do that anymore. I could never even ruffle his hair without a complaint. I just walked by him and used my nails and ruffled and scratched at his scalp and hair. I hardly got a response, besides a look of "What are you doing?" WOW! It just hit me what a hard time I used to have with getting him to wash his hair. If I would give his head a good scrub there would be major tears. He would get so mad, like I did the worst thing ever to him. It did not matter if I was gentle or really went for it, he would react the same. This always stressed the whole family.

A few weeks later, Mom said, "[Caleb] is much more tuned in to the lives and concerns of others. He asked his sister how her sleepover went. He asked his sister what she did today." Mom and Dad both have been quite surprised to see him take an interest in the activities of others.

Caleb's one-year NDD re-testing showed all of the primitive reflexes as completely inhibited, except for some minute signs of the ATNR (yet within the normal range). All of the previously erratic eye movements stabilized so that even hand-eye tracking was smooth. Caleb had one remaining postural reflex to develop more fully. Visual-perceptual and auditory processing skills were good.

Caleb recently joined a Tae-kwon-do class, and his mother shared with me how impressed she is with her son. She is excited to watch him stand on one foot as he lifts and extends the other (which he previously could not do). When the instructor gives a series of moves to be executed, her son processes the directions and is able to carry them out as directed (something he previously could not do). She notices other children who move awkwardly, show delayed responses and are unable to carry out a sequence of instructions; and it reminds her of how far her own son has come.

Caleb is now able to enjoy learning without physiological interference. His reading is better than ever, his writing is steadily improving and his processing is no longer slow. Mom started using my reading/spelling/writing curriculum as part of Caleb's fifth-grade home-school program. She brings home library books for him, and he thanks her appreciatively, because he now loves to read. In two weeks he read the first two books in the series *Warriors* by Erin Hunter. The first book was 272 pages, the second book 317 pages. Mom said comprehension is very good. What an excited mother!

Caleb's mother recently shared her pleasure at how far Caleb has come. She said she remembers when, not long after starting NDD Therapy, as Caleb's difficulties were diminishing, the stress levels in the house dropped by 50 percent. She reminisced about small things, like when he used to run into her with the grocery cart every time they were at the store. He used to fatigue intensely after a short walk and wanted to go lie down. Now he takes long walks and even runs down the street, and his mother is amazed at his endurance. Caleb participates in junior drag racing, which requires tremendous multi-tasking: precision with timing, controlling the vehicle's speed, timing brakes and turns, and awareness of other drivers. Just after he turned 11, Caleb took second place in the annual Western Conference Junior Drag Racing competition.

> *"I see other children struggling as mine did and I think, 'There's another child who needs Anna's services.'"*
> Heather and Caleb's mother

Isabella

Previous diagnosis of auditory difficulties, with prior intervention from an auditory assistance program at her school

Isabella was an extremely soft-spoken, shy girl. Her early development and health seemed average, except for severe allergies treated by a seasonally prescribed medicine. When Isabella was a kindergartener, her school discovered auditory difficulties and enrolled her in an assistance program. This continued into first-grade. Her physical and emotional health declined between the ages of six and seven. Isabella's doctor diagnosed her as having dairy difficulties; she suffered from re-occurring juvenile polyps and began undergoing annual colonoscopies. She also endured an extremely poor peer relationship with a classmate, and soon her teacher and her parents noticed a very unhappy, miserable child who no longer showed any confidence. Academically she struggled with decoding sounds in reading, although she tested at grade level. Writing was difficult primarily because her spelling was extremely poor. She struggled with multi-task activities. She could do well in math as long as it was simple and single-task-oriented. In more complicated math problems she often inverted addition or subtraction.

Isabella's second-grade teacher elected to focus on confidence-building for Isabella and encouraged her parents to do the same at home. Isabella's frustrations and anxiety showed in her piano lessons as well. Her mother said she was unable to maintain rhythm even with a metronome. Isabella was not well coordinated, yet she did not manifest significant signs of gross motor difficulties. She became dizzy quite easily, even when reading, and suffered from extreme motion sickness.

I met Isabella when she was eight years old, the summer before she entered third grade. Isabella's NDD assessment showed difficulties with balance, residual Moro, TLR, ATNR, STNR and Spinal Galant reflexes (she still struggled with nightly bedwetting), as well as underdeveloped postural reflexes. Eye movements were impaired, visual-perceptual skills were impaired, and she showed auditory difficulties. Her balance and sense of direction were significantly impaired. Isabella was obviously withdrawn, as she would not answer me when I asked her a question unless she could answer by a shake or nod of her head. When she did speak her voice was too soft and I could not hear her. She smiled and looked to her mother to speak for her. One day I watched as she and her brother got out of their car and headed for my door. The car alarm went off, and both Isabella and her brother froze in their stances and covered their ears with their hands. They stayed frozen to their spots until their mother turned the alarm off.

Isabella began NDD Therapy that summer. The following is an example of her writing skills at the age of nine, as a third grade student and shortly after starting NDD Therapy. Isabella's paper is about a field trip to a bakery (*House of Bread*).

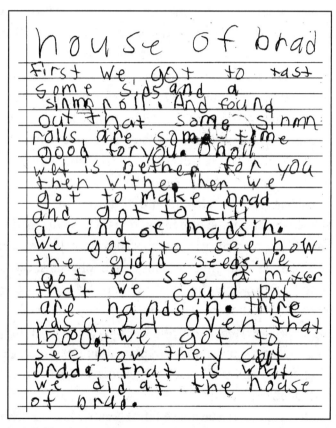

Within just a few months of starting NDD Therapy, Isabella's mother shared with me that she was "astounded at [Isabella]'s verbal expression." Isabella was beginning to share her thoughts, ideas and feelings with her mother. Some of her timidity was dissipating. Her mother said she was beginning to sing with other children in duets at church. Her parents were surprised, not only by her willingness to sing with other children on stage in front of an audience, but also by the improvement in her pitch.

The next spring, nine months after starting NDD Therapy, Isabella's teacher and parents shared observations. Her teacher noticed improvement in spelling and said Isabella was becoming more conversational. Isabella's mother said she was waking up to her alarm by herself for the first time. Her parents were delighted with her self-discipline and dedication to doing her best in school. She still struggled with playing soccer, motion sickness, reversing letters and words when reading and inverting addition and subtraction.

During Isabella's last month of third grade, her mother said the changes in the previous several months had been phenomenal. Instead of being so soft spoken that no one could hear her, she was sometimes too loud. School tests showed she was at 5.9 grade-level in reading and 5.4 grade-level in writing. All of a sudden her mother noticed improved soccer playing. She described Isabella's usual clumsy running as "running like the wind," and she played aggressively instead of hiding from the ball. Isabella's teacher described her as a model student.

One year after starting NDD Therapy, Isabella showed remarkable improvements. She said she no longer felt dizzy when she read; the Moro, TLR, ATNR and STNR were inhibited or within normal ranges. The only primitive reflex left to inhibit was the Spinal Galant. Postural reflexes were emerging. Isabella's eye movements had improved significantly, and her visual-perceptual skills were very good. Balance had improved as well as her sense of direction. She talked to me more conversationally, and I could hear her without straining. Eye contact was good. Her mother said she was now able to enjoy performing in public with less self-consciousness; her gross motor skills had also noticeably improved. Interestingly, when Isabella went for her annual colonoscopy, her mother said the doctor was quite surprised when, for the first time, he did not find any polyps.

At about this same time Isabella's mother took her off of her seasonal allergy prescription, and Isabella showed no allergy symptoms. During the previous year, changes had been implemented in Isabella's diet. Her mother had eliminated processed foods, white sugar and dairy as much as possible. She also administered high-quality daily vitamins and probiotic supplements. The following spring she added plant enzymes to Isabella's diet to further enhance the functioning of her digestive system. Whether it was the dietary changes and/or the NDD Therapy that helped Isabella overcome her allergies and polyps is not clear. Nevertheless, I think her immune and digestive systems were likely affected by the changes in the functioning of her central nervous system. The result was Isabella's health had improved, and she felt better both physically and mentally.

Isabella began and completed a 50-hour Listening Fitness Program during her summer as a nine-year-old soon to enter fourth grade. Her fourth-grade school year showed improvements in all subjects. Following is a sample of her writing skills as a fourth grader—remarkable improvement in just one year.

> The invasion mystery
> not very long ago
> there lived a little town
> Nothing ever happened
> but one day that all
> changed.
> Some animals were
> grazing peacefully When
> they started to
> stampede. They were acting
> insane. Since I saw
> this happen I decided
> to investigate. There was
> an alien sort of thing.
> It had a sticky note
> that said, "I have
> come to invade this
> planet." I could see the
> alien was a fake.
> It was made of concrete.
> It was also in a
> costume. I went to visit
> Mrs. White who is a
> costume designer, and
> fixes hemlings. She said
> she had sold it to a

Isabella

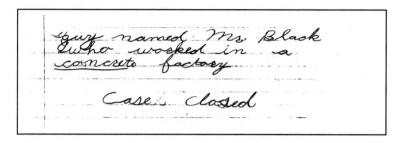

Multi-tasking was no longer a problem. Math improved significantly, and Isabella was giving speeches and presentations in front of her class. One of her presentations was so nicely done that her teacher asked her to present it to another class in her school, which she did. Her mother shared with me that Isabella now loved to perform for large groups. She was still a shy young lady, but she was no longer withdrawn or unresponsive. Her fourth-grade Colorado Student Assessment Program (CSAP) testing showed that she was *proficient* in all subjects. I tutored her with my reading/spelling/writing curriculum throughout Isabella's fourth- and fifth-grade school years. At ten years old, she began riding a bicycle!

Isabella's fifth-grade Colorado Student Assessment Program (CSAP) testing reported that she was *advanced* in all areas tested. The following summer Isabella's mother noticed her motion sickness was completely gone, and bedwetting had nearly ceased.

Isabella graduated from NDD Therapy and academic tutoring shortly before she started sixth grade. She is an A student, has been enrolled in an Advanced Learning Program at her school and is an excellent writer. When I look over samples of her work, I would conclude that Isabella's weakest subject is spelling, although she tests as advanced and excels in all of her subjects. Her sixth-grade teacher said about her writing, "[I]t's a natural gift that you should treasure." On her first trimester report card, her teacher said, "[Isabella] continues to excel in all subject areas. Her fantastic work ethic and kind personality shine a light on our classroom every day."

James

Attention difficulties and academic delay

Isabella's brother James developed early. He walked at one year and articulated beyond his years at a very early age. However, he constantly fought nasal congestion and ear infections. James had ear tubes inserted at two years of age. He disliked having his teeth brushed, and his mother fought to gain and hold his attention.

Loud or excessive noise bothered James. He covered his ears whenever his mother turned on the kitchen blender. James took a seasonal prescription for allergies and sometimes suffered from motion sickness. Academically, he was unable to remember one day what he had supposedly learned the previous day. His mother said it was quite a struggle trying to teach him the letters of the alphabet. He could name some letters one day, and the next day he would have to relearn the same letters.

I met James when he was five-and-a-half years old. My initial assessment showed significant balance difficulties, a fully retained Moro and STNR, nearly fully retained TLR and ATNR and a residual Spinal Galant reflex. His eye movements were significantly impaired, and he showed auditory processing difficulties. James could say the ABC's, but if I pointed to specific letters, he could not tell me the corresponding names. He could write his name, but his grip control was shaky. In contrast, he was advanced at math and counted all the way to 29 very rapidly.

James began NDD Therapy soon after his assessment. One month later, after showing significantly reduced sound sensitivity, he started a 60-hour Listening Fitness Program. Three months later his mother said he seemed to be staying on task a little better and was more cooperative. His kindergarten teacher said he was making better choices in the classroom, and she wasn't repeating directions as often or having to get his attention. He was better at staying on task. He was able to recognize the names of the letters of the alphabet and say them when observed randomly. James' gymnastics teacher commented that usually James mentally wandered off in class and it was difficult to get his attention, but suddenly she noticed his attention would come right back to her when she directly addressed him one time.

Distressingly, within just a few months of completing the 60-hour listening therapy James' doctor discovered a tube (thought to have fallen out) was still in one ear, and that same ear had 80-percent blockage from wax buildup. His mother and I considered this a major setback to what we hoped the listening therapy would have accomplished. James was still struggling with articulating middle sounds in multi-syllable words. When I asked him to repeat the word "auditory" he said "aubitory." We agreed to hold off on a listening Boost until after the school year ended.

Seven months after starting NDD Therapy, the TLR was nearly inhibited, and James showed some inhibition of the ATNR and STNR. His eye movements were significantly improved. His mother said he was no longer showing any hyper-sensitivity to sound; he had stopped covering his ears when she turned on the kitchen blender.

During the summer between kindergarten and first grade, James' testing showed gradual improvement in inhibition of the primitive reflexes and improved eye movements. He completed a 10-hour listening Boost while continuing NDD Therapy.

James struggled through first grade. His teacher said he was significantly delayed in spelling, reading and writing. Although his attention and focusing had improved, they continued to be areas of struggle. He still became quite tense when asked to do something with a timer. His teacher said working independently was very difficult for him. He was unable to use his time appropriately and get organized. I noticed that James still struggled with processing middle and ending sounds in reading and spelling.

During his first-grade school year, his mother changed James' diet and eliminated white sugar, dairy and processed foods as much as possible. She also began supplementing his diet with a high-quality daily vitamin and probiotics.

The following summer, James completed a 20-hour listening Boost while continuing with NDD Therapy. I began tutoring him with my reading/ spelling/writing curriculum. When James started second grade that fall, his testing showed a fully inhibited Moro reflex. The other reflexes had significantly diminished, and eye movements were improved. His second-grade teacher was the same teacher he had had in first grade, and within the first few weeks of school she noticed an amazing improvement in James' reading and writing. He no longer showed any delay at all. She was so pleased with several of his creative writing papers that she showed them to other teachers in the school and his stories were read to other classes. On several occasions James chose to remain at his desk during his recess time because he wanted to write. His mother said she was surprised one night when he sat at the kitchen table and stayed focused for about 20 minutes while writing a letter.

During James' second-grade school year he began to excel in reasoning and processing skills. He began riding a bicycle. He no longer suffered from motion sickness, and no he longer needed seasonal prescription allergy medications. His mother and I both noticed that James reacts to dairy products and performs much better when dairy is eliminated from his diet. The following spring his mother added plant enzyme supplements to his diet to further enhance the functioning of his digestive system.

When I re-tested James near the end of the school year, the primitive reflexes were nearly fully inhibited, and his eye movements were smooth and stable. When he completed the school year his report card showed above-grade-level skills in math and grade-level skills in all other subjects. He had taken a Cognitive Abilities Test halfway through the school year. Test results showed a composite score of 99 percent nationally!

James spent the summer between second and third grade in NDD Therapy and tutoring with me in writing and spelling. Shortly after James started third grade, his teacher recognized his high intelligence and responded accordingly. At the first parent-teacher conference his teacher shared that James is an "outstanding writer—clever beginnings, lots of details, solid endings ... fabulous reader with great comprehension—loves to discuss a story ... incredibly high-level thinking skills in math and great verbalization ... highly motivated." James has been placed in an Advanced Learning Program at his school and will soon be tested for Gifted-Talented abilities. One day after school James' teacher said to his mother, "[James] has continued to show himself as incredibly competent in all areas. He's a great guy!"

James' progress through NDD Therapy and the Listening Fitness Program is best described as "slow and steady wins the race." His progress was very slow but consistently showed improvement, and he finally won the race! This intelligent young boy had Neuro-Developmental Delay and auditory difficulties that contributed to significant delay in most of his subjects at school. He overcame his difficulties through NDD and listening therapies, and now his true potential is shining forth. On James' first third-grade trimester report card, his teacher shared the following:

> What a pleasure to have [James] in class this year. Those beginning-of-the-year wiggles have settled, and he has turned into a very conscientious, hard-working guy. He's a great reader, a fabulous writer, and absolutely excels in math. I think he's

being challenged in some new ways through the ALP group, the math group that works on exemplars and Jr. Great Books. He's just plain fun to have!"

"This was a very natural way to develop my children into the people they were meant to be ... it took time and patience, but the seeds were planted, and they have blossomed beyond my imagination."

Isabella and James' mother

Jeff

Symptoms of ADD (Attention Deficit Disorder)

Jeff never showed any abnormalities as a newborn or toddler. However, he was delayed at toilet training and continued bedwetting at night, even as an eleven-year-old. His mother described him as a picky eater: "He has a big appetite but eats only a small number of foods compared to the rest of the family." In first grade, Jeff's teacher wrote "Jumpy [Jeff]" on the board when the class was learning about the letter "J" because he had a hard time sitting still. He rushed through his work in order to finish before anyone else, and accuracy was not important to him. As a fifth grader, Jeff began having different teachers for various subjects. He maintained good grades, but his teachers and parents noticed swings in his performance. He would score 95 percent in one subject one week and only 65 percent in the same subject the next week. His teachers voiced concern over his impulsivity and rushing through his work. His fifth-grade science teacher knew Jeff loved her class, yet she observed very distracted behavior and a struggle to stay focused even on his favorite subject.

Jeff's parents were concerned about his academics as well. He had good grades overall; yet, because he rushed through his work, he often made a lot of needless mistakes. He often skipped words when copying, or omitted words altogether. His mother summarized his behavior in one word: "impulsive." She said, "He often does not consider the consequences of an action before he does something. He answers questions with the first thought that comes into his head, rather than giving a more thoughtful answer."

I met Jeff when he was 11 years old, during the summer before he started sixth grade. After completing a full NDD assessment, I found that Jeff had a fully retained Moro reflex. He also showed signs of Palmar, Plantar, TLR, ATNR and STNR reflexes, as well as underdeveloped postural reflexes. Although his eye convergence was good, his eye tracking movements were almost non-existent. He also showed auditory processing difficulties.

Jeff began NDD Therapy right away. Three months later his mother sent the following email:

This week I attended parent-teacher conferences at school for [Jeff]. It is the end of the first nine-week grading period. He got straight A's in all of his academic subjects. (Last year, [Jeff] got several B's - the first he'd ever had in his life). So I was very, very pleased with that ... but the big news was that his school also gives Conduct marks which basically grade behavior. [Jeff] received four Exemplary marks (the highest mark) and three Very Good marks (the second-highest mark). His teacher said that very few middle schoolers receive four Exemplaries on their report card. She had no comments that used words like "fidgety" or anything to do with focusing issues. I was thrilled.

Jeff continued with NDD Therapy and began a 60-hour Listening Fitness Program. When he finished his 60 hours, I re-tested him. The Palmar, Plantar and TLR had completely inhibited. The Moro, ATNR and STNR showed significant improvement, and the head righting postural reflexes were fully developed. Jeff's eye tracking showed significant improvement as well. His nightly bedwetting lessened to between 50 and 60 percent.

The next spring, four to five months after starting NDD Therapy, Jeff's mother shared the following:

His eating has improved. He has several new foods now and is more willing to try something new. His tastes are still for "simple" foods, but at least he has a few more foods to choose from ... baked potatoes are a recent addition to his diet that pops to mind. For years he wouldn't even taste one, then for the next several years he swore that they were awful when we made him have his "one bite." Now he thinks they are delicious.

[Jeff]'s writing has definitely improved. He enjoys writing more and is better at it. Also, his handwriting is more legible and, oddly, much smaller. He used to have big, sloppy handwriting; now he has small, fairly neat writing.

The following summer Jeff completed a 20-hour listening Boost. Shortly thereafter, bedwetting occurred about once every six weeks, and then ceased. Fourteen months after starting NDD Therapy, I re-tested Jeff and graduated him. All of the primitive reflexes were fully inhibited and all but one of the postural reflexes were fully developed (he decided to work through the last one on his own). His eye movements were smooth and stable. Auditory processing was excellent. He shared with me that he is better able to listen and follow directions, and able to complete his work in the classroom without being distracted. His mother shared the following:

> There has been an incredible improvement in [Jeff]'s jigsaw puzzle skills and interest. I first noticed it at the beach in July. He has become much better at using a combination of color and shape to determine which puzzle piece to try in an open spot. There has also been a big improvement in his desire to read for pleasure. He just read the third Harry Potter book in 4 days ... that sort of commitment to a book would have been unheard of last year.

In a recent e-mail from Jeff's mother, she said, "Thought you might like to see this e-mail I received from one of [Jeff]'s seventh-grade teachers. I hope you know that [Jeff]'s father and I appreciate all the work you did with [Jeff] to make such a letter possible."

Jeff's seventh-grade social studies teacher shared the following:

Mrs. [_____],

I just wanted you to know how wonderful [Jeff] is and how special he is to me! Each day he comes to class ready to learn and is always participatory adding his knowledge and understanding to the class discussion. Furthermore, he is such a great help! I can always count on him to run an errand or to "organize" the class. He keeps the others on track and helps me often! What a joy he is each day! You have raised a wonderful, polite young man who adds beauty to this world! Thanks so much for all that you do. I am a grateful teacher.

Two months after Jeff graduated from NDD Therapy I received this e-mail:

Dear Miss Anna,

Guess what? I haven't wet the bed for TWO months! I kind of find that interesting since I used to wet the bed a lot!

Thank you for everything. Auditory has served me well. I can focus in school better. I can write neater and I also don't wet the bed.

Sincerely,
[Jeff]

p.s. Thank you!

"I'm not the most observant of people so when I DO notice something, it's significant ... For [Jeff], however, the two biggest, significant and positive changes that I noticed were elimination of bed-wetting and more focus and concentration in general. Even if these were the only two changes, I would consider [Jeff]'s therapy to have been a resounding SUCCESS!"

Jeff's father

Alyssa

Symptoms of ADHD
(Attention Deficit Hyperactivity Disorder)

Alyssa's early development was advanced. She started creeping at seven months, walked by herself at 11 months and talked early with perfect enunciation. Her mother said she had an amazing ability to pronounce *any* word when syllables were broken down for her just once: "One of her first words was 'condensation' because she asked what the wetness on the outside of my glass was." However, she did not like to have her hair washed, brushed or combed, something that continued through the age of seven-and-a-half, when I met her. She frequently appeared to ignore her parents' requests and instruction. When her ballet teacher mentioned that Alyssa often did not respond when called upon and commands were often repeated, Alyssa underwent a hearing test at the age of three. "She passed the test with flying colors," her mother said.

Alyssa had experienced moderate-to-severe ear infections between the ages of two-and-a-half and five. As a kindergartener and first grader, Alyssa did fine academically. Conversely, she was often reprimanded for not listening in class. Her first-grade teacher suggested that Alyssa's parents consult a pediatrician about her inability to focus and get simple tasks completed. The teacher and parents completed questionnaires for possible ADHD. The teacher said Alyssa often failed to pay attention to directions when she should have been listening with the class, or when involved in her own thinking and independent work. She seemed overly interested in what others were doing, forgot what she was supposed to do after instructions had been repeated, struggled with organizing her work and was often observed fidgeting with objects such as crayons or other school supplies.

Alyssa's parents noticed problems at home as well. Her mother said Alyssa could not sit through a meal without moving around and getting up from the table. She seemed to be easily overwhelmed with large tasks and had a low tolerance for frustration. She was easily distracted and did not appear to listen when given tasks to do. She could start a task, but was quickly distracted by a toy, or a book, and would completely forget about the task. Her parents had to sit with her while she did her homework so that the work was completed. Her mother said her "nighttime routine has been the same for years ... but for months she would ask every night what to do."

I met with Alyssa when she was just past seven-and-a-half years old. After a complete NDD assessment, I found residual Moro, Palmar, TLR and STNR reflexes, a fully retained ATNR and underdeveloped postural reflexes. Her eye movements were extremely poor for her age, and she tested as having auditory processing difficulties. It was obvious to me that her attention span was extremely limited, particularly during the oculo-motor and auditory testing; she was quite fidgety and displayed excessive body movements. I wondered at the time if they were the result of an uncontrolled inattentiveness or if she was using available distractions in order to avoid specific tasks that she knew were difficult for her.

Alyssa began NDD Therapy immediately, as a beginning second grader. Within the first three weeks her parents noticed significant changes:

> She has been back to school for three days and has not been on the behavior list once. I don't think that has happened since school started. She also earned a ticket (that's a good thing) during silent reading because she was reading silently while others in her group were talking! She has suddenly offered to do household chores...[her father] claims that an extraterrestrial being has switched bodies with her ... [Her father] had the opportunity to talk one-on-one with her teacher who says that she has seen a behavior improvement.

The next month Mom shared this:

> She is no longer the emotional basket case that she was. Things seem to be improving at school. She got her 10th ticket this week (which she traded in for no homework Tuesday night) and got her 11th today! (These being for good behavior in class).

And, two months later, Mom gave another update:

> First, she had an outstanding day at swim team practice on the day before Thanksgiving. That night she was writing in her diary. The idea of a diary is one she really likes, but she usually doesn't spend much time writing in it. That night, as I went into her room she was one-and-a-half pages into her writing!! I thought she was writing about what a great practice she had, but it wasn't, it was just about her day in general!

Three months after starting NDD Therapy, Alyssa started a 60-hour Listening Fitness Program. The next month, she received a report card from school. Her mother e-mailed me and said, "[Alyssa] just got her latest report card, and she went from an N (needs improvement) to an S (satisfactory) in following instructions!"

As Alyssa completed the listening therapy, just after turning eight years old, I re-tested her. She tested as having completely inhibited the Moro and Palmar reflexes. The TLR was nearly fully inhibited and the ATNR and STNR had significantly diminished. The head righting postural reflexes were fully developed and the remaining postural reflexes were emerging. Eye movements showed significant improvement as well. She tested as able to sustain attention and focus, follow multiple directions without having instructions repeated, ignore extraneous sounds and accurately discriminate between sounds. I provided her parents with suggested follow-up recommendations so that Alyssa would not revert to previous patterns of behavior with regard to listening.

The next month, Alyssa's mother shared the following:

As far as the creative writing goes...she hasn't asked me to run out and buy her journals or diaries....BUT when she does have a writing assignment she will write freely and much longer sentences and paragraphs than she has in the past, without being asked. She continues to take the initiative to take the accelerated reader tests on her own at school and rarely gets below a 100%.

She got her report card on Monday. Still Outstanding in reading and spelling, Satisfactory in everything else. But the shocking and very exciting thing was her teacher's comment: "[Alyssa] continues to be a very pleasant, well-behaved student who has become conscientious in completing work." Hallelujah!!!

At the end of her second-grade school year, Alyssa's mother said:

[Alyssa] **loves** reading and being read to ... [Alyssa] got top in her class for Accelerated Reader and second for the whole second grade (10 classes). She has made it her goal for next year to be number one for all of third grade (and she's well on her way!).

I re-tested Alyssa after one year of NDD Therapy, and graduated her. All of the primitive reflexes were inhibited to within normal ranges, and the postural reflexes were fully developed except for one last one, which she may continue to work through on her own. Alyssa's eye movements were stable and smooth, and her visual-perceptual skills were good. She did not show any auditory processing difficulties. She no longer complains about her hair being washed, brushed or combed. Her mother said, "She is very active; we go to the pool every day after homework is done. We hike a lot, and Alyssa rides her bike whenever she can. She has asked to start basketball this year." And her first-quarter report card as a third grader showed straight A's.

Samuel

Diagnosed with SIED
(Significant Identifiable Emotional Disability)

Samuel is a little boy who manifested extreme behavior difficulties. His single-parent mother was overwhelmed with how to care for her son, and continually inundated with accusations of having poor parenting skills. Both mother and son spent a great amount of time in tears.

As a toddler, Samuel showed a weak left side, observed when creeping and crawling, and spent a few months in physical therapy. He seemed to startle easily and showed nervousness about being swung. His speech and language skills were advanced for his early years—he was very articulate and expressive. Although he was always at the bottom of the growth chart, he was a healthy child.

When Samuel started preschool his troubles began. He attended three different preschools in one academic year. Each school described him as a child who had difficulty with group settings. He became a troublemaker, distracted other children and showed feelings of being overwhelmed. He often curled up and sucked his thumb.

As a three-year-old, he was asked to leave his Montessori preschool because his behavior was too distracting for the other students. The director of the school told his mother he was not able to focus, was not ready and could come back when he showed more maturity.

The second school, a parochial school, said he was a handful. His mother was told that Samuel had a hard time listening, following directions and sharing toys. His ability to write or complete age-appropriate worksheets was practically nonexistent. He often told "bad jokes," which his mother described as "just bad humor." "His charm kind of made the teachers endeared to him as he tried to make them laugh," she said. "In spite of all his challenges, God blessed him with a bit of charm, and I think that has kept him alive at some of his schools!" His teachers were impressed with his highly technical vocabulary. A daily reward system was started wherein Samuel received lollipops for good behavior. His mother brought him to school early each day so that he had time to adjust and prepare for the classroom. He was allowed plenty of rest time in the afternoons. Behavior improved, but he still could not complete the curriculum. During the school's Mass services, Samuel curled up into a ball, covered his ears and sucked his thumb.

As a four-year-old, Samuel's behavior often seemed rude and impulsive. His mother struggled with taking him to church because he was not able to sit still or remain quiet during the services. His Sunday School teachers described him as overwhelmed by the group activities and noise levels of the other children.

Samuel's third preschool was another Montessori school. Here his teacher described him as very wiggly, noisy and as having significant focusing problems. His mother shared with the teacher Samuel's need to hold his shirt and suck his thumb when he felt overwhelmed, his need for daily naps and his need to have play time outside. One day Samuel said to his teacher, "The ears are on, but the voice is out. There is a bee trapped in my head, and it can't get out." He often verbalized, "I have electricity in my body."

Samuel's family moved, and he was transferred to a different campus within the same Montessori school. He was now four-and-a-half years old. His teacher thought Samuel might have hypersensitive hearing. She noticed he could hear a train passing nearby before anyone else in the classroom. She said he often intentionally crashed into other students and made crashing noises when the class transitioned from one room to the next. She began to move him in and out of the classroom before the other students. Samuel's afternoon naps were often two hours long. During the spring of that school year, Samuel's hearing was tested and determined to be perfect. Child Find sent an observer to watch him in the classroom. (Child Find is part of a program enacted by the U.S. Congress to identify and refer individuals with disabilities.) Samuel's mother said the observer from Child Find described Samuel as a child who had poor behavior, not disabilities. His gross motor movements tested within normal limits; sensory processing tested as within normal limits; fine motor skills tested as mildly delayed; and communication skills tested within normal limits. He was considered "Non-Disabled."

Samuel's mother asked his teacher to complete a questionnaire for my evaluation. The teacher described Samuel as follows: inattentive, accident prone, uncoordinated, easily distracted by ambient noises, easily overwhelmed, hears unusually faint sounds, needs instructions repeated, fidgets specifically when listening or speaking, has difficulty following instructions, struggles with balance, difficulty with sitting still, low muscle tone, difficulty adjusting to different environments and situations, poor sense of rhythm, difficulty getting organized, difficulty staying on task, difficulty relating with peers, learns in spurts, craves movement, speaks too loudly and mismatches his voice intonation with the meaning. She said:

> [Samuel] often makes loud disruptive noises like a car or fire engine at inappropriate times, and when he is having trouble focusing and completing a task. He has said on a few occasions he has bees in his head and we have to help with it.

Samuel's mother often received calls from the school principal. Samuel was in her office again and again because he hit a teacher, or he said he didn't want to be at school and was not going to obey anymore or he just wanted to go home. Sometimes he would snuggle up on fluffy pillows piled high in a corner of the social worker's office and say he wanted to go home. His mother often picked him up from after-school care and found him irritable and fatigued. He threw fits and often hit his mother when she pulled him away from the computer or from Lego-building. As a result, his school days were limited to half days.

I met Samuel shortly before he turned five. His NDD assessment showed full retention of nearly all of the primitive reflexes. His eye movements were extremely poor, balance was extremely poor and auditory processing skills were severely impaired. I remember asking Samuel to lie down on the floor on his back. He did as asked, but he assumed the fetal position. When I straightened his legs, he pulled them back up into the fetal position. Later, I asked him to position himself on his hands and knees as I demonstrated. He was unable to do it. He sat on his haunches and imitated the STNR position. I pulled his hips up and asked him to hold them up, and he could not do so. He immediately fell back down onto his haunches.

Samuel began NDD Therapy within a few days of his fifth birthday, during summer vacation from school. Shortly after starting school he was re-evaluated by his school for possible learning disabilities. Testing showed him to be extremely bright, above average in intelligence. It was determined that Samuel could not receive reasonable benefit from regular education alone. He was diagnosed with Significant Identifiable Emotional Disability (SIED), and recommendations were made for assistance with multi-sensory presentations through the school system. Samuel's mother asked the school's occupational therapist to hold back on specific therapies while he was engaged in NDD Therapy.

Within the first few months of NDD Therapy, Samuel's mother shared the following story:

> [A] young teenage girl frightened [Samuel] by accident while he was outside watching a train go by. In an attempt to be playful, she came up behind him and covered his eyes to make him guess who was behind him. I had seen my son's reactions to much less startling things and expected him to haul off and hit her with his bike helmet. I had seen him do this a few times before and cringed as I ran to him to try to keep him from hurting her. I was shocked that he saw her sad face as she apologetically hugged him and held his anger in and just sobbed and shook. It was the first time I had ever seen my son able to detour the fight or flight response.

Four months after starting NDD Therapy, Samuel showed significant improvement. His balance was better; he held his head straight when standing and he showed some inhibition of primitive reflexes. I received the following in an e-mail from Samuel's mother:

> I have been so excited all day that I couldn't wait to e-mail you! I am not sure if [Samuel] has done this at school before (I've never seen any papers come home like this) but he just spontaneously started writing numbers from one to 21 last night around 7:30 p.m. This "math homework" (according to [Samuel]) had to be interrupted for bedtime ... but as soon as he woke up he went right back to work. He followed me

around the house asking questions like, "Mom, how do I write the number after 12?" It was great, Anna. I had no idea he could even write numbers beyond one. He made a euro sign for a three and he knew it was not exactly right but he laughed and said it was like an "e"! The rest of the numbers he worked diligently at, ripping out the ones he did not think were "quite right" and redoing them carefully ... His numbers were inverted and backwards but very readable. He also used only one hand. His index finger was straight down the top of the marker. He was so proud—it was just awesome.

A week later, his mother reported this:

He is constantly asking about words and wants me to read everything aloud and he's actually looking at the letters trying to make the connections. It's really an awesome thing to see in him. He is able to do math in his head now; like three plus three and four plus four ... but then he tried doing six plus six and he got sixty-six. His sister said, "No, it's twelve!" And (get this) he said, "No, because three plus three plus three plus three is sixty-six!" And I thought, good logic, even though it doesn't work. He knew that two threes equaled six and that two sixes would equal four threes. He just couldn't go beyond that ... I was very proud to say the least.

Six months after starting NDD Therapy, Samuel showed significant progress at his re-testing. The Palmar and Plantar reflexes were nearly fully inhibited, eye movements were beginning to stabilize and balance had improved. Samuel's mother sent me the following e-mail:

He is counting out loud several times a day. Just this morning he was talking to his teddy bear in the car on the way home: "I am going to count to a hundred without any zeros!" And he proceeded to count to 100 skipping all the multiples of 10! He is constantly saying, "Mom, three threes equals nine! Mom! Ten plus two is twelve!"

He is reading consonant-vowel-consonant words with little effort. Last night he read a book to me (that he copied at school) that included words like "jet" and "red" and he kind of laughed at the way he had written some of the letters because he knew they were not quite right. They were all legible to me and I could see what they were supposed to be.

Tonight, his teacher gave him two pages of *BOB Books* to read for homework. He has never had homework before today. They are having him trace his name at school. [His teacher] has been very impressed with his increase in academic abilities, and mentioned today that his behavior at school is much better as well. I was shocked though, when she told me today that she expects he will be ready for first grade next year. I can't believe she said it, even now. I am so excited,

Anna. It is only a couple of months since they said his goal by the end of this year was to read simple [consonant-vowel-consonant] words and then have him repeat the year.

The following spring, nine months after beginning NDD Therapy, Samuel showed remarkable changes in re-testing. His balance was stable; the Palmar and Plantar reflexes were fully inhibited, as was the Spinal Galant. The Moro, TLR, ATNR and STNR all showed inhibition, but not completely, and eye movements showed improvement. The head righting postural reflexes were nearly fully developed. Samuel no longer showed extreme sensitivity to sound. His mother shared with me that his teachers agreed to let him move to full days at school again for the coming fall, when he would begin first grade. They thought he was ready to handle extended school days and the expectations of first grade. Mom realized that, yes, her son was behaving better and more maturely. Naps had disappeared, and the teachers began giving him higher-level kindergarten work. His mother shared this:

> I even noticed that he became more engaged with the other students around him. Before, they were more of a means to an end; if one boy had the shovel he wanted, he would befriend him so they could "play" together. Instead, I saw him emptying his backpack of special toys and giving them away to other kids when he would say goodbye at the end of the day. He would

come home with "homework"—a page of *BOB Book* stories, and he would zip through it almost effortlessly. He would also try to read all the street signs while we would drive in the car.

The following summer, when Samuel turned six, he completed 60 hours of a Listening Fitness Program. Within the first few days his grandfather noticed increased self-control in Samuel. He told me when Samuel gets emotional he "puts himself in time-out to settle down." He also noticed Samuel's attempts at reading multi-syllable words such as "classic cars." Several weeks later, Samuel's mother commented how well Samuel behaved when the family attended a wedding. She said he stayed with her while other children seemed out of control. Here are some general observations from Samuel's mother:

> Since the start of the therapy I have noticed that he is able to play a complete game of Uno with the family, or an entire board game of Junior Monopoly. I am observing that he is able to put himself into a separate room when he feels like hitting someone or throwing a tantrum. He also accepts his loss of privileges if he does act out, with less arguing; and accepts responsibility for his behavior, for the most part.

Samuel (six years old) completed the Listening Fitness Program shortly before returning to school for first grade, 11 months after starting NDD Therapy. Re-testing showed good balance and complete inhibition of the TLR. Samuel showed minimal Moro and ATNR reflexes. His ability to focus, stay on task and exhibit calmer behavior had improved dramatically. His mother said, "[Samuel] is skipping meals to learn now. We have to coax him to eat because he is so involved in his learning!"

After Samuel's first three months of first grade, I re-tested him. He showed no evidence of any early reflexes except the STNR. His eye tracking was good unless he engaged in cognitive activities. Vertical tracking was quite difficult for him, which often parallels retention of the STNR. The following day his mother met with the staff at his school regarding Samuel's Individualized Educational Plan (IEP). Samuel's mother later shared with me that the school's special education staff was amazed and pleased with Samuel's progress during the last year.

I spoke with the school social worker on the phone, and she eagerly shared her observations. She said a year ago everything Samuel did exhausted him physically. He often "seemed to be floating" and walking on his toes; his eye contact was poor; and play was difficult as he often misunderstood his peers and did not have a good sense of body space. At the end of his kindergarten year she felt he had matured enough to manage first grade, but she was still concerned. He struggled with transitions in the classroom. As a first grader, Samuel is doing much better. She said he seems excited about his work. Eye contact is good, he has made friends, his vocabulary has increased incredibly and he is more verbally expressive. He thinks things through and expresses himself well. He moves at a more normal pace. Last year he seemed "wired," and this year he has slowed down significantly. He continues to move faster than others, but the pace has noticeably changed for the better. His fine motor skills are better. He no longer wants to curl up on the pillows in her office; when he sees her he wants to talk—he shares about his friends, his family and his schoolwork. She said his presentation has matured. He currently is not quite able to keep up with grade-level activities, but he continues to improve. He still struggles with completing tasks, and he labors over writing tasks, yet improvement continues. The social worker believes Samuel's strengths are in math and science—"he is brilliant." She thinks in time language will be another strength because of his rapid increase in vocabulary and verbal expression.

Samuel continues with NDD Therapy and will be monitored for the next year or two until he is seven-and-a-half or eight years old.

"[Samuel]'s life has been truly changed ... His confidence and his curiosity have been unleashed, and I know that he will be able to accomplish whatever God puts before him because of your work."

Samuel's mother

Kaitlyn, Lynn, Rosie

Speech delay difficulties

The stories in this chapter are related because all three little girls were preschool age with similar difficulties when I first met them. None of them were old enough to have exhibited academic or behavior difficulties that could be attributed to their speech delays. Each of these girls showed initial signs of neurological dysfunction, and each of them had already experienced speech therapy, without success.

Kaitlyn, age 3

I was asked to evaluate Kaitlyn after having started NDD Therapy with two of her siblings. Her parents shared with me that Kaitlyn had been evaluated by Child Find, a community organization that identifies and refers individuals with disabilities. Kaitlyn spent time in speech therapy and was released when it seemed she had reached certain goals. However, her speech was quite delayed. She seldom talked and when she did, her family struggled to understand her.

An initial age-appropriate NDD evaluation showed that Kaitlyn had a retained Moro reflex. She started NDD Therapy at the age of 2.3; at the age of 2.11 she showed significant inhibition of the Moro reflex. She then began a Listening Fitness Program. Right away she started babbling. Then her mother noticed she was starting to place her tongue in the correct position for making the "l" sound, and she began incorporating the sound in words when she spoke.

Before Kaitlyn finished the listening therapy she was talking "all the time," her parents said. Her father asked one day, "Now how do we stop her constant talking?" Her articulation was good, and she began asking to learn sounds of the alphabet as her siblings were in their home-schooling.

Lynn, age 3 1/2

Lynn was delayed in speech and language development. She had had moderate ear infections between 18 months and two-and-a-half years of age, one with a very high temperature and double ear infection. When she began preschool, two mornings per week, Lynn was fine the first two weeks. After that she cried uncontrollably and could not be consoled. Her mother had been picking her up early so often that she finally pulled her out of preschool.

At the age of two-and-a-half Lynn was evaluated by a community "baby" intervention program. Her vision and hearing were found to be normal, and her speech and language skills showed a "lack of significant developmental delay." It was noted, however, that Lynn truncated words (removed first and last consonants) and distorted vowels. Receptive and expressive language skills were considered normal for her age. Lynn did not qualify for assistance.

Lynn's parents had her evaluated by a children's healthcare services organization two months later. She tested as within normal ranges in all areas (behavior, cognitive, oral motor, feeding/swallowing, respiratory, receptive and expressive language) except articulation. Speech therapy was recommended, and Lynn spent the next nine months in therapy. Yet her articulation remained poor.

I met Lynn when she was three-and-a-half, two months after she completed speech therapy. An initial age-appropriate NDD assessment showed evidence of a Moro reflex, and nearly fully retained TLR, ATNR and STNR. Her eye movements were significantly impaired, and she showed auditory difficulties related to sound discrimination, speech and articulation. I noticed her pencil grip was poor when I asked her to draw a picture of a person. Below is her drawing, which shows significant delay for her age (usually a three-year-old can at least draw a circle that represents the head or body).

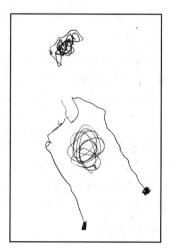

Lynn began NDD Therapy, and less than three months later her mother said, "I saw her teacher today, and she said that [Lynn] has really come into her own. She is a much happier child in school and rarely cries anymore, unless she's hurt. She's happy to be there now!"

Lynn began a 60-hour Listening Fitness Program three months after starting NDD Therapy. Before she completed the listening therapy, her mother said, "I think [Lynn] is doing much better, especially with [articulating] blends. 'Spider' used to be 'pider,' and now she says it perfectly."

I re-tested Lynn five months after she started NDD Therapy. The Moro and TLR tested as nearly fully inhibited, and the STNR showed significant inhibition. Eye movements showed significant improvement. Upon completion of the Listening Fitness Program, Lynn also showed significantly improved speech. She had begun to correct herself in articulation. Lynn was able to say the initial "th" sound in words and told stories with good detail and accurate sequence. She was able to discriminate between consonant blends as well as short vowel sounds. She no longer truncated words and could accurately repeat multi-syllable words. Amazingly for her age, she was able to stay focused and on task for 30-minute periods of auditory processing skill enhancement activities.

Five months later, Lynn's mother shared the following:

> [Lynn] is speaking very well these days; in fact, I think she has surpassed her friends of the same age in ability and articulation. The only problem now is…she never stops talking!!

Lynn was re-tested again, one year after starting NDD Therapy, at the age of four-and-a-half. She showed exceptional balance, complete inhibition of the ATNR and within normal ranges on the Moro, TLR and STNR. Her pencil grip was good, and her eye movements were appropriate for her age. Re-testing of auditory processing skills showed her as advanced for her age. She was able to draw a circle, cross, X-shape, square, triangle and diamond (advanced skills for a child her age). Once again I asked Lynn to draw a picture of a person. This time her drawing showed average ability for a five-year-old.

Her mother said,

> [Lynn] loves being read to more than reading herself. We have started her on the Stage 1 *BOB Books*

and she started to look at the pictures to remind her of the sentence which she had pretty much memorized. So now we cover the pictures until after she reads the sentence. She is doing very well! ... [Lynn]'s pencil grip problem is completely cured!

Rosie, age 2 1/2

Rosie showed mixed signs – developmental delay as well as advanced development – at an early age. She napped longer than usual for her age, walked at 11 months, talked late and showed advanced sensory-motor development. Fine motor skills seemed quite advanced, particularly with her ability to grasp and use a pincer grip. As a two-year-old she could hold a pen or marker perfectly. Yet her speech and language development seemed to be severely delayed. At the age of 28 months, her talking ability was equivalent to that of an 18- to 20-month-old. She had suffered with more than ten moderate ear infections between the ages of 18 and 28 months. As a preschool child, Rosie chose to communicate with her peers through facial expressions, gestures and pointing. When frustrated, she occasionally resorted to pushing and hitting other children.

One month after Rosie turned two years old, her parents had her evaluated by Child Find. Her hearing tests were normal. She tested as delayed in gross motor skills and speech-language development. Rosie began speech therapy.

I met Rosie four months after she started speech therapy, when she was almost two-and-a-half. An initial evaluation suggested residual primitive reflexes, and Rosie began a daily exercise to stimulate her vestibular system as well as the Moro reflex. One month later she began a 60-hour Listening Fitness Program.

Two months after starting NDD Therapy, Rosie was re-evaluated by Child Find. She tested as having improved gross motor skills, although she still struggled with balance. She was no longer shying away from crowds and was beginning to say one-to-two-word sentences. Her memory showed improvement. She had begun drawing details on faces and she was interacting with others more, showing less frustration and hitting others less at her daycare. Rosie's mother shared with me that Rosie had begun trying to count, and her willingness to try to communicate had improved significantly.

One month after completing the listening therapy, Rosie's mother shared, "[Rosie] is doing great. She is really trying to say three-word phrases; and she is nearly potty-trained, too!" Rosie's grandmother shared with me how pleased she was at Rosie's improvement in such a short time. Her aunt called me and shared the same thing. She said she was surprised one day when she heard Rosie say to her brother from a toy-riding-car, "Come push me."

Rosie returned to preschool in the fall, at the age of three. One month later her mother reported, "She is coming along amazingly!! Her speech has probably increased 75 percent by now. She is using three or four words together, and she communicates with her peers. She loves to talk on the phone!" Just recently her mother shared the following:

The one thing that amazes me is how fast she potty trained and the things that she can remember now!! She loves school, there has not been one day where she didn't want to go, never a struggle!! The most heart warming thing now is that she can say, "I love you," and "I miss you," and she communicates with her brother.

Kaitlyn, Lynn and Rosie are all functioning beautifully. I have suggested to each of their parents that they be re-evaluated at the age of five or five-and-a-half and again at about seven-and-a-half so that we can effectively monitor developmental progress. Because they showed early developmental delay, it would be to their benefit to ensure that the primitive reflexes fully inhibit, the postural reflexes fully emerge, the vestibular system functions maturely and oculo-motor and visual-perceptual abilities remain age-appropriate.

"It's amazing to think back to six months ago where she was and now how much she has improved. I think back and wonder if we never did the Listening Fitness Program, where would we be?"

Rosie's mother

Epilogue

The preceding stories all demonstrate assorted manifestations of Neuro-Developmental Delay (NDD). While each of the children revealed different struggles in varying levels of severity, each one tested as having neurological dysfunction beginning with the brain stem. Some children showed body movement and/or sensory difficulties; others had good, even athletic, coordination yet struggled academically. Some seemed to struggle only with behavior. Others struggled in every area. Labels and diagnoses differed, yet the underlying problem in each case was dysfunction of the central nervous system, beginning with the brain stem.

These children have completed (or nearly completed) NDD Therapy, and the resulting maturity in the development of the central nervous system is evident. The specific areas in which each child struggled improved dramatically, and cognitive skills surfaced or improved. Compensation techniques disappeared, and true abilities came forth.

Probably the most exciting end-result observations I have seen are the increase in reading and writing abilities and the development of a love for learning in nearly all of the children. I am delighted beyond words when parents share with me their children's comments such as, "I missed snack time because I was reading my book." "Be quiet, I am trying to read." "Why would I want to watch TV when I can read a book?" Children who at one time said, "I don't want to write. I can't write," now get excited about writing and want to share their work. I am so pleased when they bring me paragraphs, poems and stories they have written, and together we rejoice in these newfound strengths.

I am in awe of the vast number of parents who are true heroes for their children. These parents research, observe and willingly provide whatever is needed in order for their children to reach their true potentials. They act as my daily assistants, communicating to me valuable observations and insights. Additionally, these parents have become extremely committed to the therapy and are able to help me gauge the progress gained. I truly am impressed with and admire such parents. They literally give all of themselves in complete self-sacrifice as they provide for their children's deepest needs.

Do I see 100-percent success? No. Some parents decide the daily commitment is more than they can do. Some get discouraged quickly and decide this isn't working for them. Some want "quick fixes," and this is not a quick-fix program. Some commit to part of what is needed, such as NDD Therapy, but not to other needs, such as the Listening Fitness Program. In some cases I have suspected toxicity in the body and/or vitamin-mineral deficiencies, and some parents elect not to investigate further.

I have often found that if a child is on one or more medications, particularly for behavior control, the rate of progress is significantly slower. These children do show progress, but the time it takes seems to be considerably longer than for children with similar difficulties who are not on medications. I have seen a few children, less than two percent of my cases, who have genetic defects. One particular child seemed to be unusually slow at demonstrating any progress and, after further testing, it was discovered he has Klinefelter Syndrome (an extra x-chromosome). Some autistic children have specific genetic mutations. Chromosome disorders or genetic defects do not prevent progress with NDD Therapy. Progress can occur, but it will most likely be limited to some extent based on individual cases.

While not all parents are willing to pursue whatever is necessary, most are. In every one of my cases in which the parents have committed to treatment of each area affected, and have seen it all the way through, their children have experienced tremendous gains. Often there is concordant rapid academic growth as barriers caused by NDD are removed. However, it is not unusual for a child to take one to two years of follow-up academic assistance to catch up completely; again, this depends on the level of severity and the age of the child. As these children reach their potentials, some become average students, some become above average, and a few prove to be highly gifted. But all tend to have strong and weak subjects, as we all do.

Sometimes the changes in behavior and personality are quite drastic as the children mature and blossom and reveal their true abilities. When dysfunctions are worked through, confidence is gained, and a child's true personality comes forth; we can begin to see who this child is and how he or she "ticks." I found it to be a very exciting time when I began to learn about my own daughter—who she is and how she thinks. Is she still shy? Yes, but she is no longer withdrawn. Does she do things the way I would? No. Is she highly organized like me? No. Does she keep her room clean? Occasionally. Does she have the interests I have? No. If she were still school-age, would she be a straight-A student? No. Will she be an athlete? No. Is she her own person—a fully functioning, capable person with her own interests, passions and life goals? Yes! Absolutely yes! Like me, the parents of my students have been enormously excited to watch their children blossom into the people they were created to be.

Notes

[1] Goddard, Sally, *Reflexes, Learning and Behavior* (Eugene, Oregon: Fern Ridge Press), 2002, 27.

[2] Goddard, 10.

[3] Bee, Helen, *The Developing Child* (New York, NY: Harper and Row, 5th Edition), 1989, 91.

[4] Goddard Blythe, Sally, *The Well Balanced Child* (Gloucestershire, U.K.: Hawthorn Press), 2004, 29.

[5] Bee, Ibid.

[6] Goddard, 5.

[7] Goddard, 10.

[8] Goddard, 13.

[9] Goddard Blythe, 57.

[10] Goddard, 18.

[11] Goddard Blythe, 62.

[12] Goddard, 16.

[13] Goddard, 24.

[14] Goddard, 23.

[15] Goddard, 18.

[16] Eliot, Lise, *What's Going on in There?* (New York, NY: Bantam Books), 2000, 151.

[17] Eliot, 153.

[18] Eliot, 149.

[19] Goddard, 41.